PENCIL ME IN

PENCIL ME IN

A MEMOIR OF
STANLEY OLSON

by

Phyllis Hatfield

André Deutsch

First published in
Great Britain in 1994 by
André Deutsch Limited
106 Great Russell Street
London WC1B 3LJ

CIP data for this title is available from
the British Library

ISBN 0 233 98879 3

Printed in Great Britain by
St Edmundsbury Press,
Bury St Edmunds, Suffolk

Copyright Acknowledgments

Grateful acknowledgment is made to John Ferrara, Toby Glanville and
Fritz von der Schulenburg for permission to reprint photographs.
Exhaustive but unsuccessful efforts were made to find Ian Swift and
secure his permission to reprint the photo which appeared in *YOU*
magazine in 1983. Other copyrighted material printed here by
permission of *The Times* of London for "Diary" columns of Oct.
23–25, 1973, © *Times* Newspapers Ltd. 1973; *The World of Interiors*
magazine and Mirabel Cecil, for excerpts from "The Writer's Mews,"
October 1984. *Woman's Journal* published "Remembrance of
Meringues Past" and "A Traveller's Tale of the Nile," copyright
Stanley Olson, in similar form in its February and October 1980 issues.

For my sister, Miriam,
who couldn't wait

CONTENTS

LIST OF ILLUSTRATIONS

appearing between pages 118–119

FOREWORD

"She has held on to the values of our childhood with a white-knuckle grip, whereas anyone more gifted in the language of life would have released them at the very first opportunity," Stanley wrote, decrying the conventional, suburban life of one of our former Akron, Ohio contemporaries.

Like Stanley I never quite fit in with my family, my schooling, my hometown. Like him I had inchoate dreams of something richer, stranger, more unconventional. We both struck out for greener pastures, never wished to "go home again," never understood how those who stayed – literally or figuratively – could manage it. And although it seemed to family and friends that as a young woman I had ranged rather far afield, "Cousin" Stanley went off the map. I have never met anyone whose journey intrigued me more.

It was my good fortune that "the London Stanley" did not view me as a threat to his artfully crafted persona. I was not quite "family," yet more closely related than friend. While I was a mirror that reflected his past, which embarrassed him, I also focused admiring beams of light on his present; he seemed to trust that I loved the man he had become all the more for knowing the boy he had been. Perhaps he sensed that I, as a book editor, could appreciate that his creation of "Stanley Olson, Esq." was his most wonderful work of art.

INTRODUCTION

By the measures of the medical and actuarial professions, Stanley Olson was born and died prematurely. By his own measure, he was born at least half a century too late and on the wrong side of the Atlantic. His world view, taste and manners, sensibility and imagination, his appearance and preferred milieu were more properly those of an avant-garde Edwardian gentleman.

At the age of twenty-two, Stanley set about rectifying Nature's error: he would create himself anew – live as if born without parents, siblings, family history and religion, midwest education and cultural trappings – would craft his own life and make it beautiful, suitable, altogether fitting to his temperament. And he would stick by it uncompromisingly – to the death.

Generous with the gift of his company, a very social animal, Stanley was nevertheless a secretive man. He kept his American life and his English life quite separate. Though he saw his family in the States or in London every year, they were not privy to his inner life nor his social life (though it was they who footed the bills for most of it). And his English friends knew precious little about Stanley's youth in America. Few had met his brother and sister; none had met his parents. Most were unaware that Stanley was born a Jew; it simply did not come up. He refused to talk about his boarding-school years at a military academy, and said little about his time at Boston University. It seemed to them as if the real Stanley Olson had been born in 1969, when he moved to London and transformed himself – thoroughly, wholeheartedly, impeccably – into an Englishman.

With vast numbers and separate circles of English friends, Stanley was privy to much gossip and many secrets – who was doing what with whom, and where (occasionally, his flat was a trysting place for couples who mustn't be seen together in public) – but he never divulged to friends his own intimate relationships. Aside from one short-lived, unofficial engagement, his amours, if any, were a closely kept secret.

Only in 1986 when his friends gathered around his hospital bed, where he was unable to make proper introductions because a stroke had interdicted speech, did most become aware that they shared a mutual friend if little else. Housekeepers and shopkeepers, writers and painters, dukes and duchesses – their diversity was equaled only by their devotion to this talented, eccentric, somewhat mysterious young man.

The grandson of penniless Jewish emigrants from Russia, and the son of a man whose success was in the hardworking, philanthropic Horatio Alger mold, Stanley's adopted English life – stylish and literary – was alien to most of his family and childhood friends. As a boy he did not exhibit the outward signs of brilliance and precocity that might have alerted them to his future distinction. Top marks in school, talent on a musical instrument, athletic prowess, leadership qualities – all eluded him. He was labeled an "underachiever," a cute clownish child.

Very few people who had known him in childhood saw him later, in his second incarnation. To most of these relatives and family friends, Stanley came across as charming, witty, impeccably turned out, but rather snobbish and a bit of a dilettante. Yes, they knew he had become a writer and produced a couple of biographies, but not many had heard of the poet Elinor Wylie, and the style of his book about portraitist John Singer Sargent was a bit recondite – challenging.

They didn't take him quite seriously. I was among the few who did.

———

Our friendship began in Akron, Ohio, in the early 1950s, in a huge warehouse filled with radio parts and related inventory stacked on high metal shelves and moved by forklift to the shipping room from which it was sent around the country. We sometimes played there on weekends while our fathers worked; they were business partners and our families were so close that Stanley, his brother, sister and I called each other "cousin."

There followed years when we saw little of each other – he went away to military school, I went away to college and married – but in the mid-1960s our friendship resumed and blossomed in Boston, where Stanley had come to attend the university and I lived with my then-husband in an apartment at the foot of Beacon Hill. Once again Stanley and I could play together, but now as two adult escapees from Akron relishing our long-sought freedom.

Soon I moved west to faraway Seattle and Stanley moved equally far, but in an easterly direction, to England. Nearly twenty years passed before the next reunion, but our long, rich exchange of letters and the reports of family members and friends who visited him in London prepared me for the Stanley I would find there.

It felt as if little time had passed since our last meeting in Boston. I found not a "new" Stanley but the *real* Stanley: the imago had emerged from the chrysalis. He wined, dined, wheedled, advised and encouraged me; and most of all he honored me by asking that I edit his biography of Rebecca West, the monumental project on which he had just begun work.

*

Written off by the medical experts as fatally premature at birth, Stanley's hopeless beginnings echoed thirty-nine years later, when he was felled by a massive stroke which at first seemed fatal. He triumphed once again by living three and a half years, during which he could neither read nor write and his speech was radically impaired; yet he had lost not a jot of his intelligence, his memory, his mischief or his charm.

I went to see him every year during this period. On my visit in the winter of 1987, six months after his stroke, San Pellegrino and barley-water had replaced the ubiquitous late-afternoon champagne (though remarkably he remembered the select aged Irish whiskey I had enjoyed the year before and promptly thrust a glass in my hand). And his pleasure from tobacco was now strictly vicarious – head tilted back, a look of ecstasy in those long-lashed blue eyes as he sniffed his guest's cigarette smoke from across the sitting-room. But his sweet-tooth and appetite for rich food had *not* been subdued by the stroke or his will-power, and he insisted that we dine lavishly. Demands for "More news! More stories!" punctuated the courses, uttered with his old dictatorial brio. When I forgot to frame a question so that he could easily respond, his brow bent and I watched a brief, silent struggle. Then, "I know but I can't say it," uttered crisply and followed by a bemused chuckle, as if he were as surprised by his inarticulateness as I was.

During the night of December 9, 1989, two months after my last visit to London, Stanley suffered a swift and fatal stroke. I flew back for the funeral and, since his brother and I were the only family members present, I felt compelled to address the assembled English mourners, most of whom were strangers to me personally though the names of many were well known from books I had read. My nervousness about taking precious minutes of the short time allotted for eulogies to talk about "the American Stanley" was unfounded: the morsels I delivered about the first half of Stanley's life were hungrily seized upon by those who had known him during the second half. At the reception at Claridge's that followed the ceremony I was showered with gratitude and deluged by questions.

By a strange symmetry, my friendship with Stanley ended in a warehouse similar to the one in Akron in which it began. Amidst the audio components and shipping cartons of brother Norman's thriving distributorship in northern California stood a tall heap of Stanley's earthly goods, wrapped in gold paper for the voyage between continents: his Empire furniture, his library, and his file cabinets containing letters, diaries, the collection of small notebooks in which he drafted his biographies, and a welter of his published and unpublished articles.

As literary executor for Stanley's estate, I foresaw months of bittersweet pleasure as I sat in the warehouse reading and sorting through Stanley's very private life. Within days I found myself laughing more than crying. Stanley's personality – not only as serious writer and complicated man, but as comic writer and quirky human being – fairly leapt off the pages I held in my hands. It seemed selfish to keep this to myself.

[The attentive reader will note that spellings and usage in this memoir veer from American English to British English, with occasional appearances of hybrid forms that Stanley used early in his London years. Since "bilingualism" is inherent to the story, it seems natural to reflect it in the text rather than to impose an artificial homogeneity.]

PART I

THE AMERICAN YOUTH
(1947–1969)

The only relation we have with the past is that we – and me in particular – avoid it like mad. Someone else was living all those years ago in Akron and Boston, not me. What a blush the thought brings!

Stanley to Phyllis, 1975

When Sidney and Miriam Olson met with the doctors who delivered their second son and third child, born two and a half months early, on June 8, 1947,* they were told he could not live; he weighed less than three pounds. "Rest. Take a trip. Try to forget about this baby," the experts said. The Olson grandparents offered to take care of the death formalities when the time came, while the stricken parents followed doctors' orders and left Akron for a long drive to California. The day they arrived on the West Coast, the grandparents telephoned to say the doctors' prognosis had changed – the baby would survive! Miriam and Sidney sold their car to the first person who would take it, and rushed to the railroad station to catch the fast train back to Akron.

Baby Stanley Bernard Olson spent the first two months of his life in an incubator at Akron City Hospital, deprived of sensory stimulation and direct human contact. His future need for sensuous fullness – often to the point of surfeit – most likely began in that place of sterile emptiness. Isolated at birth, a "special case," he spent much of his short life as an exception to the rule.

Transported by ambulance and accompanied by a registered nurse, the tiny infant finally came home to join his

---

*Most of the London obituaries gave 1948 as Stanley's birth year, as did the dust jackets of his books. He knowingly submitted the wrong date to his publishers – typical Stanley-mischief – thereby indulging his habit of self-creation.

parents, his brother Norman (aged five), and his sister Arlene (aged two). The Olson house, the right size for a family of four, now became cramped by the introduction of an invalid baby and his full-time live-in attendant who remained for a year on round-the-clock duty administering droplets of formula whenever the baby would take nourishment. But the regimen succeeded: the baby thrived. And as an adult, when Stanley assumed control of his life-support apparatus, he retained certain elements of this extraordinary first-year environment: the enriched atmosphere and nutrients, the barriers to physical closeness, and the ability to attract "care-takers," people who would sustain him on his difficult way through life.

Stanley came from money – "new" money and hard-won. An American bootstrap-success story, his father's business began informally in the late 1920s when the teenaged Sidney and his brother Irving began repairing neighbors' radios in the garage of the family home. Their father, born Frank Olshanitsky, had escaped the Tsar's army (into which Jews were drafted for up to twenty-five years and given the most menial jobs) by swallowing lye; he had the roughest voice we children ever heard. He left the Pale of Settlement (the area of Poland and Russia where Jews were permitted to live) in early manhood and emigrated to America, where he took what he thought was an "American" name, Olson. He learned the machinist's trade by closely observing the skilled workers in the machine shop where he held his first job in America, as janitor. Later he started a barber shop and then a one-man printshop. There was never enough time to learn English properly and he was a terrible speller, so it is remarkable that he achieved a modest success as a printer. Frank and his wife Rose, another steerage arrival in "the land where streets are paved with gold," raised five children in Depression-era Akron.

When the brothers exhausted Akron's supply of replacement radio parts, Irving took the Olson savings, went to Chicago, and brought back enough parts from the distributor to meet their own needs and to resupply the other Akron repair shops. Before they knew it, the young Olson brothers had become distributors themselves. Eventually Sidney went on the road in a car fitted with shelves to hold the minuscule radio parts. He drove a big territory – Ohio, Pennsylvania, West Virginia – and was frequently away from home all week. He also managed to attend and graduate from Akron University and to marry Miriam Klein, descended from Hungarian Jews.

When the war ended and the demand for consumer items – radio tubes, hi-fi systems, transistor radios and then televisions – skyrocketed, the Olsons bought a warehouse, stocked it full of repair and replacement parts, and set up a small retail outlet and a vast mail-order business. They were among the first US businessmen to foster trade ties with Japan in the 1950s, providing Japanese manufacturers with designs and specifications, then importing finished consumer electronics products to America for sale at the ever-expanding number of Olson stores. Some forty years after it began, when Sidney effected a merger with a giant corporation, Olson Electronics stores stretched across the nation and its catalog reached hundreds of thousands of people around the world.

With the business thriving and three growing children, in 1950 Sidney and Miriam Olson bought a one-acre lot on Delaware Avenue in Akron's best neighborhood, not far from where the Erie and Iroquois Indians once portaged their canoes. Stanley grew up in the large, congenial house they built, set well back from the tree-lined street. He was healthy but "very skinny and the worst eater imaginable," sister Arlene remembers. Apart from chocolate and other

sweets, the only foods he liked were hot dogs, plain ham-
burgers and fried chicken. (It is unlikely that a raw vegetable
ever crossed his lips, even in his gourmandizing adulthood.)
His mother prepared two menus for the family – a regular
dinner for four, and a special dinner for him, a privilege that
innumerable cooks and hosts were to grant him throughout
his life. Thin-as-a-reed Stanley gained weight; from the onset
of puberty, excess pounds were a permanent burden.

He was visually acute and conscious of style and ambience
even as a very young boy attending children's parties. When
taken on visits to friends' houses, he noticed the decor and
furnishings and was alert to what they might reveal about
the owners' personalities – revelations he was quick to share
with family members on the return home. One had to be
sharp and on one's toes at the family hearth; the Olsons
– grown-ups and children alike – were verbally quick and
highly critical, and teasing was a favorite form of social
exchange. A compliment when someone looked especially
attractive might be tendered as: "Are we in danger of your
becoming well-dressed?" Arlene says: "Any member of our
family is capable of attending a dinner party and being as
gracious as anyone else, but next day giving the others a
withering critique, whittling everyone down to toothpick-
size. The *real* masters – Stanley became one – could reduce
someone to ashes."

Stanley could well hold his own in the family bantering,
and as the "baby" he got away with a lot more than Norman
or Arlene. Busy and preoccupied parents tend to pay more
attention to disciplining older children and let the younger
ones figure things out for themselves. Third-child Stanley
observed the consequences to his siblings when they mis-
behaved, and learned to circumvent the obvious pitfalls.
Impishness and indirection worked well; so did quiet,
stubborn persistence. And when the mischief was clever
enough and didn't actually harm anyone, his parents might
pay attention and even find it charming. He was fond of Josie

Mae, who served as maid in the Olson household throughout his childhood and could be persuaded to keep silent about pranks and misdeeds. He was afraid of Andy, the family's big brown poodle, and showed as little promise of becoming a dog fancier as of becoming a gourmet.

Though not devoutly observant Jews, the Olsons felt a strong affiliation with the Akron Jewish community and the newly established State of Israel. (After Sidney's retirement from business in 1971, he and Miriam gave much of their time and wealth to Jewish institutions in America and Israel, where they were awarded medals and honorary degrees for philanthropic activity.) The family belonged to the Reform synagogue and the Jewish country club in Akron, the hubs around which their social life revolved.

I have only dim memories of the grinning, gap-toothed boy who pinned the tail on the donkey and slathered cake icing on his face at our family birthday parties. Stanley first registered with me as a real character, a distinct personality, at a dinner-dance the Olsons held to celebrate his bar mitz-vah. Dancing with thirteen-year-old boys does not usually appeal to sixteen-year-old girls, but Stanley's sophisticated patter during our clumsy box-stepping fascinated me. What a curious mix of boyishness and worldliness! Giggly, sweet, bright-eyed and mischievous; yet amused by and ironic about himself and his world in a manner I associated only with grown-ups. Unlike me, Stanley could laugh at himself; he had a precocious sense of the absurd that saved him from arrogance then and always. No matter how "grand" he became, he had an uncanny ability to puncture pomposity – his own and others'. Now he pronounced the party "a bore" and we retreated to a quiet corner of the Rosemont Country Club to regale each other with complaints about hometown, family, school and life in general. He was being sent off to military academy and I was stuck in Akron for two more years of high school. We agreed that life *had* to be more exciting and attractive elsewhere, and that we wanted to go "there."

Akron (Greek for "summit," so named because it commanded the highest point on the Ohio-Erie Canal route) held few attractions for us as we were then, and less for the adults we would become. A blue-collar factory town, the "Rubber Capital of the World" in our youth – home to Goodyear, Goodrich, and Firestone (where Clark Gable once clerked for $95 a month) – it is now one of America's "rust-belt" cities. No tires roll out of Akron anymore; nor does the foul-smelling, sooty black smoke. The first quick-cooking oatmeal in the world was milled in a long-gone factory across the street from the old Olson retail store, and the silos that once held Quaker Oats loom today over the former Olson warehouse (now the Sidney L. Olson Research Center of the University of Akron) across the railroad tracks. Classical concerts, circuses and National Guard drills all occurred in the same space – an armory. If Stanley and I had known then the work of social satirist Lenny Bruce, we would have roared with laughter at his description of a smaller but not dissimilar Ohio town: "You go to the park and see the cannon, and you've had it. You go to the five-and-ten, look through that for a while. That's the end of the day. They've got one Chinese restaurant in town, it serves bread and butter, cottage cheese, and Fig Newtons for dessert."[1]

The nearest big city, Cleveland – an hour's drive from Akron – did not nearly satisfy our craving for grandeur, but it did possess two world-renowned cultural institutions, the art museum and the symphony, that influenced us for the rest of our lives. The Cleveland Orchestra under George Szell was a musical treasure, and their concerts occurred not in an echo-filled armory but in an acoustically fine European-style domed auditorium, under a simulated sky of midnight-blue sparkling with electric stars.

All the Olsons liked music, but none seemed to *need* it quite as Stanley did. On Sunday mornings his father's hi-fi system poured forth "light" classics. The third child's early taste was more high-brow, and he never could bear "that loud shaky music" Arlene and most every other young person of our generation rocked to. Music, and especially opera later on, opened his romantic imagination and offered a route of escape if the difficulties and demands of childhood reality pressed too hard upon him. ("Nobody ever said a thing they meant, or ever talked of a feeling they felt, but that was what music was for." So said the pianist heroine of *The Voyage Out*, whose author's work would in time help lead Stanley into a very different life.)[2] He developed a large record collection and listened with intelligence and love; at thirteen he was as effusively opinionated about musical compositions and performers as he was at thirty-nine.

Sidney and Miriam had few worries about their two older children's academic progress – Norman would soon start university after graduating from a prep school in Pennsylvania; Arlene lived at home and attended a private girls' school. But at age twelve Stanley seemed the cuckoo's egg in the family nest. His school grades were abominable, he didn't pay attention, couldn't concentrate, and in no way conformed to family expectations. Even his summers at Camp Wingaroo were a disaster: he found the weather too hot and muggy, the food awful, and participation in organized games and team sports undignified. "He was never like anyone else," his mother told a London friend of Stanley's years later. "If everyone went to the left, he would go to the right. If everybody were climbing the mountains, he would go down into a hole."[3]

The standard battery of intelligence and aptitude tests revealed no inherent problems; it seemed that all this child needed was structure and discipline. Stymied about how best to implant these qualities in Stanley's character, his parents now made a radical move: at the same time they were preparing for his bar mitzvah – the initiatory ceremony marking his full admission to Jewish manhood – they began paving the way for his admission to what many Jews considered the alien, probably anti-Semitic, environment of a military academy, a sort of toney reform-school where rich gentiles sent their wildest, most intractable boys to bully them into manhood.

In the fall of 1959, when Stanley was twelve, his father wrote to the Culver Military Academy in Indiana: would they consider admitting Stanley one year hence, when he would be ready for eighth grade? "He is immature relative to his classmates," wrote Company Counselor Colonel Moore, after Stanley attended a preliminary summer session, "and his immaturity prevents his attitude and interest being much more than superficial." It took a bit of parental persuasion, but Culver admitted him on probationary status. Hoping that the military men would do for their son what neither they nor the Akron public schools had the patience to do, the Olsons settled Stanley at Culver and drove back to Akron.

So began Stanley's five-year career in Company A, where he distinguished himself by frequent semesters on probation ("he is in academic danger"), grades of F and D in military training classes ("he is a poor shot"), lack of school spirit ("does not concern himself too much in the Company . . . carries out his duties faithfully, although does not take too much initiative"), and a personality sufficiently winning to persuade the authorities to continue accepting his hefty school fees ("Stanley is a hardworking, earnest boy").

This "earnestness" at the beginning of his cadet career was perhaps genuine, more likely feigned. It was certainly short-lived. He loathed the place and resented being there, but he had plenty of time to learn the ropes, assess how much (or how little) he could get away with (selling his uniforms to obtain ready cash was *not* acceptable), and to develop the inner strength and skills at manipulation that would help him survive with strong personality and amiable nature intact.

The colonel's regular progress reports to the Olson parents often mentioned Stanley's inappropriate "playfulness" in class, which interfered with his academic achievement, but his problems with reading were so severe – today he would probably be diagnosed as dyslexic – that his mischief-making alone cannot be held to account for them.* He placed far behind his class in reading speed and comprehension. Even when he was seventeen and about to graduate, the embryonic biographer whose subtlety of style and depth of insight were to earn reviewers' praise a dozen years later, elicited these worried comments from teachers: "Stanley needs to read extensively. He needs further work in comprehension (especially in making inferences)."

When the time came for special spring ROTC training, the Culver folks were prepared for artful dodgers, and Cadet Olson looked like a prime suspect, complaining about allergies to horses and pollens. He had written his family doctor in Akron asking him to persuade the Culver physician to excuse him from horseback riding and from maneuvers that involved what he called "sleeping and rolling in grass." Not yet a master persuader, he overstated his case, exaggerated the rigor of the training, and lost. Culver's physician accused him of misleading the family doctor about the so-called "maneuvers," and charged him to participate "regardless of discomfort"; he prescribed a higher dosage of antihistamines.

---

*Dyslexia is a cognitive disorder that some scientists believe results from a delay in neurological development, which in Stanley's case may have been complicated by his premature birth. According to *The Oxford Companion to the Mind* (OUP, 1989), dyslexia is not caused by intellectual inadequacy, inferior teaching techniques, or emotional resistance to learning, but its practical manifestations – difficulty in learning to read, slow reading speed, erratic spelling, and deficits in written language – are often seen as "educational failure" and its victims often develop emotional problems as a consequence.

Stanley's letters home were poignant confessions of laziness and lack of effort. Yet they also hint at a method of dealing with conflicts, especially with his parents, that he eventually mastered. By volunteering self-criticism he might steal their thunder. By accenting his difference from Norman and Arlene, he might play upon their sympathies and earn special indulgence; after all, the very fact that he was alive was something of a miracle.

> You have good reason to be ashamed of me for I am very ashamed of myself. Why can't I be smart like Norm and Arlene? In all my fifteen years on earth I have never brought you a bit of joy only sorrow and embarassment [sic]. I am not fit to be your son. I do nothing right as when I told you I'd work. What did I do [but] loaf [and] make a fool out of you and myself. My teachers tell me I'm smart but when I find this to be true it will be a cold day in July. Please except [sic] my apology for being the most greedy person in the world. I will try to give instead of take so much. I'm sorry I really am. Love Stan.

Midway through his third year at Culver, there was reason to expect improvement: "New excellent teachers in replace [sic] of bad ones," he wrote. "This is what I really needed, patient, understanding teachers. The ones I had in the past called me an 'idiot' and 'half wit.' " He entered a poem in the school literary magazine, and a clay sculpture of a woman's head in an art show; he said he would rather go to a summer art school than to Europe. "I have become extremely interested in writing. It has so much zest and action just as creative art work. I'm writing a paper on Henry James. I really find it fascinating. I read *Gone with the Wind* by Margaret Mitchell. It really is good. I suggest you read it."

But by the end of the year, despite his new teachers, Stanley was clearly behaving badly, had lost all cooperative spirit and was unhappy. His chewed fingernails were bloody and infected. The colonel cited "apathy" and "inactivity." His father replied that over the summer he planned to employ a psychologist to help find out "what it will take to motivate Stanley."

Even the grimmest reports of the boy's inadequacies and failures included mention of his "faithful participation" in Art Hobby Club or work in the theater stage crew. He practiced regularly when he took piano lessons, and his French teacher said he enjoyed the language "for its own sake, displaying much enthusiasm throughout the year." And though the event went unrecorded in the Culver bulletins to parents, Stanley conceived a lifelong grand passion when his music teacher introduced him to opera. But these were, after all, educational "frills" – not what people sent their sons to military school to learn.

The summer he turned seventeen, before his final year at Culver, Stanley made the "grand tour" of Europe, the first and only time he traveled with a group and didn't complain about it. There were girls everywhere, and he noticed. "I ate dinner at the hotel [in Austria]. The meal was miserable because a good portion of it was spent looking at a beautiful girl. It turned out she was engaged." He swooned over Paris, Venice and Rome, and so much regretted leaving London that he wrote: "The Channel is now making me wretch [sic]." He was beside himself over his first experience of live opera. Full pages of his travel diary show bright red "Wow!"s – especially after he saw *Aida* at the Roman Baths of Caracalla ("I went out of my mind") and *La Traviata* in Florence ("The opera was stupendous! 12 curtain calls and roses").

Back down on the farm after Gay Paree, there were few bouquets for Stanley from the colonel, who reported minimal participation in the key curriculum: "I'm afraid he is spending most of his time in the Art Studio. He is quite a good artist, as you know, and he is undergoing some instruction on a non-credit basis. He feels that his art portfolio will help him in his entrance to college."

Admission to university loomed as a formidable challenge. While Arlene toured colleges with her parents, seeking the one that most appealed to her, Stanley wrote: "I'm sorry, I can't be too selective on the school I go to for I will jump to get into any." Biology, especially genetics, was anathema to him: "Major Miracle [the teacher's actual military rank and surname!] suggests that if it is not absolutely necessary Stanley should drop science at this time."

Not surprisingly, when the end of his five-year ordeal approached and graduation ceremonies were just around the corner, Cadet Olson had an "improved outlook on life," according to the colonel. "Stanley's attitude about the conclusion of his math courses is a good indication of why he did not do better: he does not like Mathematics. I sincerely hope that Stanley will discipline himself to work on present tasks more consistently in his future work, for he is sure to have some unpleasant tasks, perhaps even more unpleasant than Mathematics."

Stanley placed 149th in his graduating class of 182. He received a standard congratulatory letter from the Culver superintendent, a retired United States Air Force major general: "I know that you are fully aware that you are indelibly stamped as a Culver Man. This in itself gives you a status which commands respect." At the ceremony, diploma in hand, Stanley broke rank as the marching cadets skirted a bush beside the hot dusty parade ground. When the Olsons joined the swarm of parents rallying to congratulate their sons, he was nowhere to be found. He had gone to his room for a nap.

At Culver Military Academy Stanley won the second crucial battle of his life – this time for the survival of his spirit. Against overwhelming odds – learning disabilities, failure to meet any measurable standard, the miseries of adolescence – and from a milieu that tried to mold him into something he could never be, he emerged with ego battered but intact. Neither Jewish nor gentile rites of passage into manhood had succeeded in giving him an acceptable identity; he would have to fight for it in his own way, with the weapons at his command: persistence, determination, and his parents' money, which could buy him wings to fly out of the cage of conventions. Rather than outright rebellion against the constraints of school and family – a strategy that risked total isolation and abandonment – he adopted passive, sometimes devious, methods for bending the world to him. He intercepted the hurled epithet "Different" and turned it to his own devices. In later life he never wished to speak of his old battle wounds.

When Stanley showed up at the door of my Beacon Hill apartment in 1966, he looked to me like most of the other New England college-types who overran Boston – slightly scruffy, dressed in the standard button-down shirt, corduroys and tweeds. But the resemblance stopped there. Ebullient, witty, sweetly bossy, loaded down with records we simply *had* to listen to, he took charge of that visit and the many afternoons and evenings we enjoyed thereafter.

By this time he had spent over a year reveling in the heady atmosphere of the East Coast and his newly won freedom from the constraints of Culver, about which he said nothing; no scars were visible. Meanwhile I had been roving from coast to coast with my new husband, and had adventures to recount that fulfilled Stanley's and my old longings for escape from Akron to "there." Although he had managed somehow to get himself admitted to Boston University, class-attendance seemed to take low priority in his life (his college transcript clearly reflects that); but since some years earlier I had passed much of my own time in Boston haunting the Isabella Stewart

Gardner Museum instead of my college classrooms which were adjacent to it, I was hardly one to discourage his truancy.

We went gallivanting around the city, to Symphony Hall, the Museum of Fine Arts, the Gardner Museum and the Boston Public Library – sites that later held great significance for him as repositories of Sargent paintings. In those days, however, we looked and listened with disinterested pleasure, Stanley a vibrant, sensuously alert companion.

At a time of life when most people have bosom buddies and move in cliques, Stanley assembled whole circles of friends that rarely intersected; he moved among them as his interests and moods shifted, a pattern that continued throughout his life. "I remember going to birthday parties where there'd be twenty people, none of whom I'd ever seen before, but they were all Stanley's *best* friends! So few of us knew so few others. It was like a Venn diagram – only a minute space where the friends actually crossed over."[4]

He was a distinct presence whenever and wherever he appeared. "He was eccentric even then in the most delightful way," says one close Boston friend. "He had such a passion for words and language and literature, and he'd often bemoan the 'crass stupidity' of most Americans – their lack of intellect and class and culture."[5] Another relished Stanley's pronouncement on the conversation of dull people: "When lacking content, add volume."[6]

Although I knew he had other friends, Stanley made me feel as if I were quite singular among them, and he introduced me to only one of my "rivals" – a budding poet and fellow Ohioan whose father had been serving a life-sentence after a highly sensationalized "murder-among-the-socialites" trial. Stanley, compassionate and efficient, enlisted my help in sequestering his friend from the throngs of reporters who were about to descend after F. Lee Bailey, the famous Boston criminal lawyer, secured the father's acquittal and release from the penitentiary.

None of Stanley's friends in Boston, regardless of their

circle, were spared uncontrollable outbursts of The Wagner Obsession, which had taken root at Culver and grew like some rainforest plant to luxuriant, fantastic proportions. ("By 1979 I have seen *Tristan* 42 times," he wrote; Wagner's death date was noted in each year's diary.) But for a while it was superseded (in conversation at least) by The Leontyne Obsession. During one season when the great diva was at the height of her career, he sent a note with a bouquet of roses to her dressing-room after *every* East Coast performance, and attended as many as he could travel to, always in the hope of meeting her in person. Finally, in New York, he got his wish: La Price invited him backstage. It was a high point in his life. Many years later he reminisced: "I found the tape of Price's opening of the new Met! 1966. I will never forget it. Poor thing, now her voice is gone."

As an amateur pianist who took music (but not opera) almost as seriously as Stanley did, I received a heavy dose of his proselytizing. He insisted that I listen with him to Mozart's *Magic Flute* (so easy to like, he said, that it would convert me to opera if anything would); Britten's *War Requiem*, which he loved more for the Wilfred Owen text than the music (Vietnam weighed heavily on our conscience); Leontyne Price singing *anything*; and Wagner, interminable Wagner. He never relinquished hope of recruiting me into the ranks of Wagnerians. Stanley said I condemned Wagner-the-composer based on Wagner-the-man; I said the despicable man maundered on too long in his music.

We had few disputes about literature, however. Stanley held forth on the glories of style and sensibility in *To the Lighthouse* and other early twentieth-century English novels I had yet to read, and he waxed eloquent on the merits of Henry James, pointing out that I lived on the very street where James had situated *The Bostonians*. I lent him some volumes of Camus; he liked *The Stranger*. (If I had known then of his reading problems at Culver, I would have been astonished at this repertoire.)

He never talked with me about girlfriends, nor did he invite me to his shared living quarters in what his sister called a "nightmarish" old frame house where he had painted his bedroom black and had a bathtub so grimy it matched the walls. Stanley's private life, then as in the future, seemed irrelevant, off-limits to conversation, not because he *wouldn't* talk about it but because one felt that only his public life mattered to him. (Even when in London he became the most hospitable of men, his inner life was a closed book. "After a highly enjoyable evening," Michael Holroyd recalls, "I would come away with an occasional sense that the sunlight faded when he was left alone and some obscure melancholia descended."[7])

Stanley's obsessions and pleasures cost money, more than he could afford on his allowance for living expenses. But why spend cash on such things as laundry or flowers, underwear or books, when with charm and masterly manipulation one could open charge accounts? If business proprietors in the student-infested city were wary of extending him credit, then he would go instead to shops that served only the carriage trade; the merchandise and service were far superior there anyway. When he left Boston for England, and his creditors eventually tracked down his father in Akron, Stanley was thousands of dollars in debt all around town.

After his second year in Boston, I bade Stanley farewell as he launched into a summer journey that broadened his interests, consolidated his aesthetic opinions (and his verbal expression of them), further opened his eyes and ears, and revolutionized his gastronomy.

He spent three months in Taiwan, Thailand, Hong Kong, and especially Japan, where his parents and brother had paved the way with previous visits and he was welcomed by his father's Tokyo business associates. "The day I arrived we conversed at Ito-san's office, where he had dinner brought up of hot-dogs, so the transition would not be too great."

His energy was immense. Despite the heat and humidity, he visited temples, pagodas, gardens and museums, and became so competent at leaving behind the official city tour guides and locating off-the-beaten-path sights that he found himself playing a reluctant Lowell Thomas to groups of tag-along tourists. But he just as often erred and got lost: "I went to the wrong train station – typical!"

The Wagnerian marathons had got him in shape for five-hour performances of Kabuki and Bunraku, which he adored ("I'd go every night if I could"), and he arranged to have lessons in sumi drawing and koto-playing. He made friends on boats and airplanes, and filled his address book with names of people he could call upon from New York to Hong Kong.

Gregarious and open to every new experience, he sought others' opinions and spoke forthrightly about his own. While touring Hokkaido University, he "happened to run into" the Social Problems Committee, with whom he "talked philosophy and Vietnam for over 4 hours"; none had yet encountered an American *opposed* to the war, he said. (Weeks later these abstract discussions took on a fearful reality: en route to the temples at Angkor Wat, he had a stopover at the Saigon airport "which is blown up once every 6 months or so." He watched as twelve planeloads of American soldiers landed; never before had he so appreciated his student deferment.) After he left the philosophers he went to another nearby university and had "a private recital" of piano and art songs. Back in Tokyo he went (uninvited) to the University of Arts: "I sat in on 2 hours of a Japanese music lesson of shamisen and koto. Both very fine. From there I went to the voice dept. and sat in on a voice lesson of a Nillson [sic] type soprano who was singing Mimi from [La] Bohème. [The teacher] assigned her 'Salce, salce' and I had a mini-argument with him for she just did not have a true soprano voice – it was more mezzo. I left after that."

When he learned that the Frank Lloyd Wright Imperial

Hotel was soon to be torn down and replaced with a twenty-story, modern hotel, he was outraged. "I registered a strong complaint with the manager," he wrote his parents. "He was callous as a stone! Ass! I hope no one stays there." Before this "gorgeous building" disappeared, however, Stanley was sure his parents would understand if he "stretched his budget" to spend one night. (In Osaka, where he had no guidebook to give him clues to prices, he checked into the Grand Hotel, "mainly because I liked the idea of saying 'Grand Hotel' to the taxis.")

He delighted in shopping and selecting just the right gifts to suit his family. To Arlene he hinted about his present for their father, who believed in art-for-art's-sake when it came to gifts: "It's very beautiful and it's not useful, which makes it in Dad's class." To Norman, who had recommended that he visit the Taiwan art museum, he wrote a scholarly disquisition on Chinese bronzes and porcelains and said he was sending him a 250-page book he had just read on the subject.

Traveling independently for the first time, he took full advantage of the fact that he could stay where he pleased and didn't have to leave cities he loved just because a tour package or a bossy escort said so. Consequently his itinerary and budget were a shambles, and his parents were alarmed. They were not to worry, he wrote: "At least I am of some use." Happy for a means of reciprocating his Japanese hosts' hospitality, and for the rare opportunity to assist in business, he was proofreading English translations of operating instructions for Japanese electronics gear headed for the American market. When he came upon packing cartons designed for Olson goods, he wrote his father: "You are developing an extremely high style line of merchandise yet the boxes are garish and overdone. I would like to talk to you about it."

Money, after all, was meant to be spent, and Stanley had wrested full educational value from the trip. "I tried to economize but could Adam when he was in Eden?"

When Stanley returned to Boston, he placed in my hand an Asian cookbook in barely comprehensible English with somewhat more illustrative photographs by Prince Sihanouk. He had sampled every sort of cuisine, he crowed, and found it delectable. Would I please search out lemon-grass and other exotica (for Boston) and prepare his favorite dishes? No more nursery-school tastebuds; Stanley was now a gourmet, and to the array of pleasures (and expenditures) he had enjoyed before his trip, he could now add fine dining. When he outgrew my culinary repertoire and those of his other friends, he charmed his way into the television studio where "The French Chef" cookery program was produced; after the cameras switched off, Stanley joined the select group who feasted on Julia Child's menus.

His attendance record at Boston University did not keep pace with the improvements in his palate; he skipped so many science classes that he risked expulsion. But he never played hooky from the classes taught by Professor Millicent Bell, a noted Henry James scholar whose influence on him was incalculable. (She was awed to discover when they got together in London years later that Stanley could quote verbatim whole sentences from her lectures.) One of her courses – "The Modern British Novel" – so stimulated him that he achieved the only A of his university career; but more significant was her role in the intensification of his affinity with Virginia Woolf and his fascination with the Bloomsbury group.

Given his grades and attendance record, the chances of getting into graduate school looked even slimmer than they had years ago when he met with undergraduate admissions officers at Culver. And now the stakes were higher: even student deferments were on shaky ground; if he were not in school at all, he faced the strong possibility of being drafted.

One day in his last semester at Boston University, Stanley

called on Professor Bell at her office. "We had become intellectual friends," she recalls,

> talking, sometimes for hours, about the books we were reading in class and about others that I urged him to read or that he had discovered for himself. He never did speak much about his pre-college years, his family, his home – except to vaguely indicate that these had not provided much preliminary to what interested him so much now. His impulse seemed to be to get as far away from such things as possible – and so I was not surprised when he told me that he wanted to go to England to study Virginia Woolf and Bloomsbury, which we had talked about – in class and out – a good deal.[8]

She wrote to a colleague at the University of London recommending Stanley as someone "of unusual promise." In short order he was accepted for enrollment at the Royal Holloway College in the fall of 1969. A tutor would direct his graduate research; he would not have to attend classes.

Professor Bell's support of Stanley never ceased. After publication of his Elinor Wylie biography and the announcement of his Guggenheim fellowship for the study of the life of John Singer Sargent, she nominated him for election to Boston University's Collegium of Distinguished Alumni. "It gave me particular pleasure to see the University acknowledge the distinction achieved by this graduate who had not been noticed in his college years, except perhaps by a very few, or even, possibly, by no one except myself."[9]

Stanley's extraordinary luck with graduate school extended to his military prospects as well. In the 1968 draft lottery, his birth date was the 366th number drawn (leap year); the odds of his being called up were next to nil.

Over the school holidays in the winter of 1968–69, Stanley went to London to scout for lodgings and meet his tutor. He did not know it at the time, but he was going home.

PART II

THE ENGLISH GENTLEMAN
(1969–1989)

My former student and friend had astonishingly transformed himself into an accomplished professional writer and, even more amazingly, an Anglicized gentleman-aesthete who was a favorite of the London intelligentsia.

Millicent Bell, after reunion with Stanley in the early 1980s

BREAKING IN

*Life consists of the personal experiments of each of us, and
the point of an experiment is that it shall succeed. . . . No
doubt I'm rough still, but I'm in the right direction . . .*

Gabriel Nash in Henry James's *The Tragic Muse*[1]

L ike Henry James's baroness, for whom "the social soil
on the big, vague [American] continent was somehow
not adapted for growing those plants whose fragrance
she especially inclined to inhale and by which she liked to
see herself surrounded," Stanley required a smaller, more
circumscribed land in which to cultivate his talents.[2] He
became a pioneer in reverse: early Americans went west to
make a new life; Stanley went east, and determined that for
him it must be the last frontier.

His slate was rubbed clean. "When he turned up in London
he came as if from nowhere. He was a mystery figure."[3]
Even his surname helped to disguise his actual background
("Olson – he must be Swedish," a new acquaintance was apt
to say). He had a prescient sense that England contained the
raw materials he required to forge a new self, make a new
beginning, and that here he could most readily capitalize on
his natural resources: force of personality, instinctive style
and attention to detail, sharp intelligence and powers of
observation.

During the time of his great transition, Arlene served
as Stanley's bridge between continents. With his sister he
felt a comfortable camaraderie, a trust and closeness that
he enjoyed with no one else at home. Norman, five years
his senior, seemed very much the "older brother," almost

a father-figure, remote by virtue of age and temperament. As the middle child, a sweet and pretty girl, much favored by her parents and very close to them, Arlene was ideally situated to be stateside sounding board and intermediary for her younger brother overseas, especially when he had money worries. With her he could test new ideas of himself, confess his troubles, boast of his triumphs, and take the measure of the ripples he was making (for good or ill) in the familial pond.

She had visited him frequently in Boston, accompanied him to London on the trip just prior to his move there, and shared his excitement about the prospects ahead. Always she respected the boundaries of his privacy, did not probe his secrets or taunt his misdemeanors. Like him she knew the rigors of graduate work (she was pursuing a Master of Fine Arts degree, on the way to a Ph.D. in Art History), was romantically unattached, loved to travel. And like him she craved chocolate and felt self-conscious about her weight (a preoccupation of every member of the family).

Until she married (at age thirty-four) a decade later, in 1979, Stanley wrote to her at least twice a month, often illustrating his letters with caricatures of his chunky body – a pig wearing a necktie, or a coat of arms for the "House of Oink," with crest of knife, fork and spoon under the motto "You're fat! When do we eat?" He reported wearing Beatles-length hair because "it makes me look thinner." His early letters reflect the typical goofiness and mood-swings of youth – exhilaration and hubris, self-criticism and defeat, romantic crushes and social fears. At no time, however, did he mention loneliness or homesickness. He did not feel them; he had found his true home. The only thing he seemed to miss was his record collection, and he made elaborate pleas for family members to hunt down and bring particular recordings when they came to visit.

His first London digs were too modern to suit him – "It's like being in Scarsdale, but of course there is far more taste here" – though he liked the fact that the block of flats was "full of really attractive females and since I live on the first floor what could be more convenient? I read for at least six hours in the park almost every day. To be honest I really don't know how I liked Boston so well when there are places in the world like London." He found the climate rather trying: "The weather here is keeping my health at a good steady even cold. Ha! Central heating indeed. The only thing that's centrally heated is my spine and that's with layers of fat."

Within three months he moved to Hertfordshire, within commuting distance of London, where he assumed a friend's lease on "a period cottage with thatched roof, leaded glass windows and ¾ acre of garden on a stream bordered by trees. Quiet and beautiful," he wrote Arlene. "It's like a Brontë novel come to life. I love it. I'm becoming a real country-ite. I hate the city." This proved to be a short-lived country idyll (and his only paean to the bucolic life), since there were problems with the lease. Furthermore, his parents came to visit and what Stanley found romantic and quaint, they found shabby and isolated; he was back in London within weeks, in a bed-sitting-room near Manchester Square where he remained for nearly a year.

He made friends with others in the building – including a couple of Americans – and even resuscitated his limp Culver tennis game. "I have a huge match in Regent's Park tomorrow, replete with white trousers, sweater and blazer. I'm going to take up cricket." Next would be Wimbledon, "to eat strawberries and cream while watching the tennis matches in a seat next to the Royal Box."

Between relocations and tennis games he worked diligently on his thesis, entitled "A History of the Hogarth Press from 1917–1923: A Biographical Study, with Critical Discussion of Selected Publications." Leonard Woolf, concerned about Virginia's fragile mental health and anxious to find some occupation that would relieve the tension of her novel-writing, had taken a lease on Hogarth House in

Richmond and, in 1917, bought a small hand-press "with the object of printing short pieces of merit which might otherwise not find a publisher, and printing them with as much style and taste as they could summon."[4] To everyone's surprise, what began as Virginia's occupational therapy evolved into a thriving commercial enterprise. Stanley followed the course of the early glory-days by reading the work of Hogarth authors in chronological order and writing up material to send to his tutor.

Over time many dyslexics learn to circumvent or compensate for reading difficulties, and the mature Stanley was a vigorous exemplar of that phenomenon: he digested books as if they were chocolates, and amazed his friends by remembering even the details of what he read. The translation of lucid thought into coherent writing remained a struggle, but that too grew easier with practice, and a bevy of loving friends and editors seemed always on hand to sort out the spelling and syntactical confusions.

After a stint on Katherine Mansfield he said his thesis was "turning out to be a mini-Eminent Georgians, as everyone comes off very poorly both through my style and by my interpretation of their F-upped psyches." He raved about Virginia Woolf's early novels and railed against Leonard, whose recent death and complicated will engendered frayed nerves among the Hogarth staff and difficulties for Stanley in pursuing his research. "When I left them I was so furious I ate a whole Old Jamaica chocolate bar," he wrote after one harsh encounter.

The staple ingredient in what he casually labeled his "neurosis-eating" was sugar, usually chocolate. His desk drawers were littered with picked-over boxes of sweets whose provenance over the years reflected the evolving grandeur of his taste and extravagance, from Cadbury's to Charbonnel et Walker. To demonstrate his love for and solidarity with Arlene during her Master's exams, he made the supreme sacrifice and gave up his then-favorite strawberry chocolates, begging her to notify him promptly of the end of her ordeal so that he could cease his self-imposed privation.

Despite the confusion at the Hogarth Press, he attracted a devoted ally – his first close English friend. Gill Coleridge, Hogarth's publicity director, cleared a work space for him in her crowded department, and when later she became a literary agent Stanley became her first client. (Their birthdays were within days of each other, and perhaps it was again a desire to demonstrate affection and solidarity – and to give an excuse for joint celebrations – that led him capriciously to shave a year off his own life to make their birth years match.)

After months of slogging through musty files at the Press and piles of volumes at the British Museum, he felt discouraged:

> I seriously have to question whether or not I am Ph.D. material, and when I see those hunchbacked bug-eyed sloppy-lipped scholars at the BM I can only tell myself I'm not them and they, *they* are the doctorate scholars. I don't want my epitaph to read: "Found melted into the blue leather chairs at seat T13, Reading Room, BM, with eyes shooting marbles over the blotter and fat fingers stuck to a pen."

He leavened his study activity with intensive bouts of opera attendance: "Am going to see *Salomé* with Grace Bumbry who does a full-front nudity scene in the Dance of the 7 Veils. Too bad my seats aren't closer. Yay for Grace." He joined The Friends of Covent Garden to get a discount on opera tickets, and planned to see twelve performances in three months – no doubt rationalizing this first of many binges by the fact that it was a "bargain." "Leontyne Price is singing 6 Trovatores and I have tickets for all – to say nothing of Wagner's Ring cycle." He notes an irony of scheduling that puts the arch-anti-Semite's magnum opus onstage during the Jewish High Holidays, but says he will be "in staunch attendance." "Saw *Siegfried* 3 times in 5 weeks. I go to a concert at least 4 times a week and then that doesn't seem to be enough. Quiet night at home seems a thing of the past I'm afraid!"

A primary benefit of living in England was the relative ease it afforded for making pilgrimage to Bayreuth. He was so exhilarated by performances at the Wagnerian shrine that when he returned to London he "could only wonder what I could add to the world and came up with a big zero." The only drawback was that to hear Wagner sung at Bayreuth he had also to hear German spoken in the hotel and restaurants, and he hated the language: "Asking for brown bread sounds like some volatile threat."

Many of the erstwhile quiet nights at home had been spent in the company of his upstairs neighbor, Tish Lampert, a bright, talented, wild American girl who was trying to make a career in acting, singing, photography, producing records – anything creative that would pay the rent on the Stanton Court bed-sitter and keep her in hip London.

"Stanley and I had only a handful of English friends at the time, and the fact that we were both American drew us together even though we were very different types. I wore risqué clothes and was chronically late for appointments. Stanley was always on time and dressed as if he were going to his London club."[5] But they shared a taste for sarcasm and verbal jousting, and teased one another to the point of ridicule. "The search for the perfect jibe preoccupied us all day, so that when we got together in the evening we'd be ready to do battle. He had the sharpest wit I've ever known, and if his day had gone badly he got even more biting and sarcastic."

In this testy way they earned each other's trust and affection. She called him "Stanlet" and he had a long string of nicknames for her. They dined in each other's rooms, listened to music, watched television, and confided their intimate secrets, fears, wishes and dreams. "We were best friends," she says, "at a most crucial time in my life, and he opened my mind and heart to many 'human' things."

One evening, a couple of months into their friendship, Stanley closed and locked the door of his room:

> He said he'd like me to stay the night with him, that he wanted to have sex with me, that he'd never had that experience with a woman he knew, only with a prostitute in Boston.
>
> "You *paid* for it?" I said, kidding him to mask my surprise at his proposition. We bantered a bit in our usual way and then I said no. I adored him, but I didn't want to change our platonic relationship.
>
> I think he guessed beforehand that I would turn him down, and I'm not sure whether he was setting himself up for disappointment – which would be typical Stanley – or if he was relieved and thought, "Well, now we've got *that* out of the way . . ."

Years later Tish regretted her refusal. "He needed me. He needed to overcome his doubts and fears. He had a gift for alleviating other people's fears, for making things seem not quite so scary, but he himself was a very frightened person – fearful of his body, of his mortality." Fascinated by suicide, romanticizing it, he imagined aloud to her the details of Virginia Woolf's death; she was not surprised that Wagner's morbid love/death themes appealed to him so strongly.

They carried on their friendship as before. He might go into a long sulk from time to time, but that was nothing new. "He would make almost a game out of staying angry – seeing how long he could keep from talking to you. He could be terribly immature." Most of the time he was his usual helpful, bossy, funny self, excoriating her taste in men, warning her at the onset of ill-advised love affairs, and then bailing her out when they crashed. He promoted her photographic career by introducing her to the reclusive eccentric, William Gerhardie, an aged author whose picture she took and then sold to a London newspaper. And he invited her to his favorite opera, *Tristan und Isolde*, where with tears rolling down his cheeks he proposed marriage. She was touched and flattered, but felt certain that his tears and proposal were inspired by the Wagnerian passion onstage rather than down-to-earth romance at Stanton Court; she turned him down.

They drifted apart during her second and final year in London. "I looked upon my time in London as an escape, a romp. For Stanley it was a serious time, the beginning of his future."

The day before Stanley's first birthday in England he wrote Arlene: "I'm depressed because tomorrow I will be 23 and I've been a failure most of that time. Worst of all I've had advantages far above most everyone else and yet I'm still nowhere." Nevertheless he planned to celebrate with "a nine course gourmet meal complete with langoust[e] and Beef Wellington and – and I will wear white tie no less. I'm looking for a *used* one, 1930s preferably."

While implying economy with his search for secondhand formal wear, the incipient dandy was simultaneously visiting custom clothiers, as a "favor" to a friend from Boston who had once lived in London and asked him to "keep up" with Harvey & Hudson, Longmans, and other expensive shirtmakers and tailors. He was beginning to formulate a principal tenet of his *modus vivendi*: doing things for others that give them pleasure offers one license and justification for satisfying one's own hedonistic desires.

Shortly before Stanley went to England, his parents bought a Rolls-Royce. When his mother scheduled a London visit, he planned to welcome her in the style to which she was accustomed. "Dad sent me some money to hire a car for Mir when she arrives at the airport and I think I can wangle an old

1940 Rolls limousine for her at a reasonable price. Don't say anything. I want it to be a surprise." The scheme went awry.

> Of course I was at the airport for four hours this morning as Dad gave me the wrong flight number and I had no idea when Her Nibs would arrive so I had to hope for the best. I had to let the chauffeur go as the car was costing a fortune, so Mir couldn't taste the luxuries of a limo. Her first words were: "Look at that hair!"

Despite the ups and downs of his academic work and his three changes of lodging in the space of one year, he could write in August 1970: "Yesterday is the first anniversary of my residence in England – who would have ever thought I could last it out and make it my home: I'm pleased that I have."

———

A month after his London anniversary, claustrophobia set in. "I have to get out of living in one room. It's falling into rack and ruin and the landlord won't fix it up." Now, in one master stroke, Stanley satisfied his domestic requirements *and* his Wagner fetish: he and a friend called Howard leased a large West Hampstead flat, with four bedrooms and a garden, on a road called "Parsifal." To celebrate he marched over to a New Bond Street stationer and ordered "posh new paper to write all the old Bloomsburyites on," thus launching another lifelong obsession. (Eventually, nothing met his exacting standards but hand-laid paper, in a range of sizes and custom colors to suit every mood and occasion.)

He felt pleasurable surprise at the emerging quality of his thesis, and was clearly overjoyed at his gleanings from reading and research. "Did you know that Dora Carrington was Dorothy Brett's 'virgin niece'? – that D.H. Lawrence was particularly good at hemming? – that Katherine Mansfield

plagiarized Tchekov? and Virginia Woolf made good jams?
I hope it's news to you."

He sent Arlene a formal, printed invitation to join the
Chrysalis Club, "a new organisation of (20) creative people
to share their art and ideas with other interested writers and
artists . . . to stimulate constructive criticism (if desired) and
general interest as well as creativity." In an appended personal note he said he was a founding member of the club
and that she was privileged to be one of only three overseas
members solicited. So far "the only problem is that most of
the members – 12 all told – are so fucking brilliant I end up
saying zero. I have in the last week written 10,000 words so
it has at least stimulated me."

A dose of Fantasy, administered as a stimulant to hard
labor, rarely harms the patient, and it is likely that the
unnamed members of this club-without-an-address were
creatures of Stanley's fertile imagination. Certainly there
are echoes of Virginia Woolf cranking out pages on her
letter-press in his statement that he was "learning the printing
trade" so he could print Chrysalis materials. In any case, the
scholarly engine revved to full power: "On Friday the Diary
and Letters of Dora Carrington came out," he told Arlene,
and

> after skimming it I found five rather major factual errors. I
> composed a letter to the editor, David Garnett, but decided
> that nothing could be gained by starting up a fuss just to prove
> how erudite I am, so I will go in on Monday anonymously
> and point them out. I guess I must know my material to be
> able to do that, or else I'm just plain arrogant.

Mundane reality intervened by way of sporadic onslaughts
of visitors from America: "I am beginning to feel that I am the
stock in a pressure cooker and all these people keep toppling
in on me." Some toppled more clumsily than others: "If they
think they are the crème de la crème of Akron I'll happily be

a pimply boot-black any day." But nothing provoked a more serious confrontation with reality than a parental visit, during which he was certain to be chided for regularly overspending his allowance while making no arrangements for gainful employment and apparently planning to stay indefinitely in England. After one visit with his mother he reported "some rows" to Arlene:

> I told her at least three times I've applied for jobs, and have been offered two in the U.S. but I wanted to hold out for a position here! Of course not holding my degree doesn't help getting firm dates as to when I will be employed. I can't believe she thinks I have no plans at all! . . . Anyway, I don't think she is pleased with me. The blow of blows came when she said I am a Hard Head. I hope I never hear that expression again as long as I live!!! I never think I've been as furious as when I heard that singular epitaph [sic] placed after my conduct! I often don't think I fit in with our family. I think I am so dissimilar. I really feel too often that I am just put up with and that I was never really meant to be! I am not feeling sorry for myself but that is the way I feel sometimes.

He neither yielded to pressure nor succumbed to self-pity, but rallied his spirits through work and mischief:

> I'm in a live-wire mood; I'm at work on Logan Pearsall Smith, a man little known and vastly under-rated and delightfully humourous [sic]. While reading the *Who's Who 1944–46* (my favourite pastime anyway) I came across the mini-biographies of the Sitwells. As "Recreation," Osbert writes: 'Thinking for myself – all other activities in abeyance for the duration of the war.' You should get out the old volumes and read them; I was reduced to a quivering heap of mirth. I rang the phone number listed [in the old *Who's Who*] for Logan P-S to inform the subscribers of their famous number. Needless to say they were not over-pleased. I also went into the most matronly-stuffed branch of [the drugstore chain] Boots I could find and asked *voce loude* for Cat Poison; I was caned from

the shop by an indignant old-age pensioner.

The weather was so fine today I went to buy seeds for the garden. Among the delights are summer scented stock, Blood-red Wallflower, Giant Sweet Peas, French Breakfast Radishes and none other than Sweet William and Sweet Something else whose name escapes me. I will plant them next week; I'm determined to have the messiest garden in the street. All the rest are so well-groomed you would puke. . . . I found a hedgehog last week and he is now in repose in a tomato crate outside stuffing himself with bread and milk and apples.

His confidence grew like the garden, as did his critical capacity and his willingness to exercise it on anyone whose opinion he disagreed with. But he softened the impact with humor, sending himself up at the same time he put someone else down, in this instance Arlene:

Doing hand-to-hand combat with a bilberry vine [that threatened to overtake the flower border] makes me think of your gushing praise of Gertrude Stein's Autobiography of A.B. Toklas; God how could you like it? What total rubbish. I don't ever recall hating a book more. Did I recommend it to you by chance? If so you are reading words from the world's largest hypocrite.

He deigned to acknowledge that "Stein's *Making of Americans* is quite astute, however" and went on to say: "If you like Evelyn Waugh, and I know you do, read the man from whom he admits that he learned all his tricks – William Gerhardie. Read *Futility*; I was holding my sides. When you come to England you can meet him as I know him fairly well. He is a man of enormous charm and wit – something like me."

Stanley had met Gerhardie – and many other writers as well – through the good graces of up-and-coming biographer Michael Holroyd. Since Gerhardie had written the first book in English on Chekhov, and Stanley struck Holroyd then as "a figure from a Chekhov play – very much the perpetual student," he thought the old man and Stanley would amuse one another, as indeed they did.[6] (In his youth in St Petersburg, Gerhardie was considered the dunce of his family but held a very high opinion of himself; he performed "withering renditions of Wagner on the piano"; and in old age subsisted on a diet of meringues – just a few characteristics that endeared him to Stanley, who later wrote about him in the *New York Times Book Review*.)[7]

Now the Parsifal Road establishment geared up to reciprocate the Holroyd favors. Stanley was about to give a dinner party, his first in London, and he was so excited that he gave Arlene a running account over a three-week period:

Michael Holroyd is coming to dinner Sunday with Philippa Pullar who is an expert cook! I'm scared shitless. Wanna come? I could use your facility in the kitchen! Howard (my flat-mate) said he'd help me, as he will be here too and doesn't want to choke. Holroyd menu: boeuf Stroganoff, caramel oranges, vichysois (sp!) and after that a stomach pump and a bee-line for the toilet. I really can't believe they accepted my invite. "We'd love to come" – you could have knocked me over with a feather!

Holroyd and Pullar were at supper chez Parsifal Rd. I was so nervous I was shaking like a leaf. I spilled half a bottle of sherry I was so scared. Philippa Pullar wrote me yesterday to say she had a very good time. He is the only man – Holroyd – I've ever met that is perfectly comfortable with his brain: no need to parade his knowledge or upstage etc. anyone else. She is the sexiest middle-aged – 30 – woman I've ever seen. Every word is like a mini-orgasm – she's splendid. I really am taken by her! We talked about penis-shaped breads, as she wrote a book [*Consuming Passions*] on phallus cookery!! He signed my Strachey [*Lytton Strachey: A Critical Biography*] and I piled on the praise which he so aptly deserves.

I just spoke to Philippa Pullar (the Michael Holroyd household) to give them some bad news: I found an error in his *Strachey* and I couldn't bear to write him about it as it is the second one I've communicated to him. He's doing a revised edition now so I am saving him some work. Anyway, her charm has won me over again: to communicate a simple thing we were on the 'phone for 45 minutes!!!

Years later Philippa and Stanley collaborated on a menu to be published in *Food & Wine*.[8] Fortunately, the magazine requested only the recipes; the ordeal of preparation, which Stanley describes in the following piece, shows that his future mastery of the dinner party came not without a painful apprenticeship.

COOKING WITH PHILIPPA[9]

It must have been the closest day in London in a decade. The sky was unrelieved Portland grey. I had to get from Montagu Square to Barnes Common – about six miles on a diagonal line through the heart of town – carrying various foodstuffs for twenty people, a liquidiser and six bottles of champagne, while attempting to control a very uncooperative spaniel.

Philippa and I had decided that I should arrive at 10 a.m.; dinner was at 8. My departure had been prefaced by at least twenty long, detailed telephone calls; I am a fuss and Philippa is cool, but unwilling to compromise. "Dinner parties take *all* day. Let's make it a big one and probably the last one for a very long time," she said. Prophetically.

While I was tumbling across London, crowded into a taxi and jammed in traffic, P was making the two courses that need time to reach perfection – a jellied consommé and coffee granita – the first very complicated and the latter deceptively simple. But both required a fridge in perfect order. As the temperature outside climbed, and more and more things were stored inside, the fridge developed very worrying symptoms.

The addition of six champagnes was the last straw.

It was 10.45 a.m. My spaniel shot through the front door, nearly overturning a very complicated flower arrangement in the hall, and flew to the kitchen in the back, petrifying the cats along the way. Fur flew; P was not pleased. It wasn't a good start. I wanted to keep an eye on the dog and insisted that he stay in the kitchen. Anyway, I am allergic to cats. She relented, and then I got annoyed with him getting trod on. With the dog safely locked in the study and the cats too scared to return, we rolled up our sleeves and set to work. We sat down at once. There was a lot of noting things down on paper, a lot of counting on fingers, a lot of unproductive small-talk. We dismissed those tasks we would not have to face for at least six hours. That left the main course to prepare – gnocchi – which neither of us had done before. It would take, we calculated, about two hours what with note-taking, measuring, debating, arguing, tasting and cooking. There would be an hour for lunch, time for tea and time for a rest before people arrived. A myth.

No two people can be more ill-suited to cook together than P and I. She is boldly optimistic while I am fiercely pessimistic. Her optimism brushes aside the need to have all the correct ingredients, materials and skills – she just gets on with it and is inevitably successful. I take unnecessary care to make things precisely as they *should* be; P asks what *should* means. If we worked independently her recipes could never be repeated and mine would be in a permanent straitjacket. And if we worked alone we would be overtaxed and overtired.

We decided to use her kitchen, mine being so small one has to open the window before sneezing. P's is large and peculiar. There are no handles on the kitchen taps; one must use pliers instead. Her collection of saucepans is very odd; all of them have lost their flat bottoms and their lids. The cooker is mounted into a table far too low in the centre of the room, and every electrical gadget has assumed a life of its own and won't work without one's indulging its idiosyncrasies. But these are details one quickly gets accustomed to, overlooks and rather loves, with time.

We had decided on a vegetarian menu. P had just come back from India. My resistance was not great; I had just come back from my bank. And we based it on what was readily picked out of P's garden, with a bit of help from the greengrocer. We devised a recipe for gooseberry ice and decided to try it out. I boiled the gooseberries and went to look for the sugar. It was getting very close to noon. No sugar. "Really, P, you can't possibly have no sugar?" "Those children," she shrugged. "Try ... honey." The honey was poured in and the green pulp pureed, tasted and detested. "What now? What can I do?" Any alcoholic flavouring was out. India. P looked out the window wistfully. "Add some elderflower." It made the thing.

The weather was becoming more menacing, darker, hotter, closer. We had a conference while the potatoes for the gnocchi boiled, and cooked a bean stew for our quick lunch. A little wine. Our conference drifted away from cooking. Where would everyone sit? Two tables, one of them a children's paper-pasting table, would do the trick. It was going to be a tight fit. "Is X coming? Alone? And what about Y? Have you heard anything?" I asked. P shrugged. "I'll know at seven-thirty," she said with astonishing confidence. "Just late enough to drive anyone crazy," I muttered.

The potatoes were done and mashed. "You kept back the skin, didn't you?" said P unhelpfully. "Yes." That one monosyllable fired back so quickly and so ignorantly led me to spend three quarters of an hour retrieving thin peel from ten pounds of mashed potato. Not a pleasant occupation. It took vital time which we did not have.

P hates making dough. I am not fond of it, but I remembered the tomato consommé. I did it, slowly. It was now quickly approaching four o'clock. P flew to the preparation of the spinach filling for the gnocchi. Like lightning she chopped, mixed, seasoned. "Could you just hand me that parmesan? It should be on the sideboard." It wasn't. It wasn't in the larder either. The nearest shop was a twenty-minute walk away; the car was broken down. In any event neither of us had the time. P's children were conveniently away. Then fortune smiled. The doorbell rang – it was someone for P's son, with a motorcycle. He was forced to run this mission of mercy, but neither of us were too confident. He set out and it began to rain. We talked about other things, nervously. I returned to the dough. P prodded the granita and examined the unsetting consommé. I complained a great deal; flour billowed everywhere. P rushed over with a damp cloth. I was not enjoying myself and my dog was trying to tunnel out of the study. It was time for his dinner and the cats looked mournfully in through the kitchen windows. We must be mad.

The parmesan was very long in coming. The rain, I said. The fool, P said. Everything was poised for its arrival. The spinach filling was ready (but not enough – "Can't be helped," P announced dismissively), the dough ready to be rolled, and we were sitting down. Then the bright spark among us remembered the tomato sauce. "Now where are those tomatoes?" I asked, rummaging in the vegetable basket. "I thought they were on your list!" "I thought they were on *yours!*" The panic was obvious. Tins were retrieved from the larder, but there were not enough. We will just have to be miserly and measure each serving with great care. The sauce was made with an infinite number of adjustments.

It was now 4.50 p.m. and still no cheese. The consommé was not setting at all. The fridge was getting no cooler though it was set at "freeze." We hunted for table service for twenty. "But it might be twenty-three or twenty-four," I reminded P helpfully. "I'll know at seven-thirty," she reminded me helpfully. The sink had managed to flood the drawer that held the knives, forks and spoons. Mad drying. Even madder search for chairs. Some were hauled from the potting shed, but they had no seats. We stuffed in some cushions. They will do for thin people. That leaves me out. Candles. Mats. Salt cellars. Pepper mills. Cheese plates.

5.15. The cheese arrived. Hectic scramble to put the gnocchi together. We did it badly and had to do it again. It was complete.

6.10. The hunt for soup cups was on. Then P remembered that two of the guests *hate* tomatoes, and tomatoes figured in two of the courses. She grabbed the saucepan with the remains of our lunch – beans and lentils – tossed in some stock and then handed it to me to liquidise. I didn't have the heart to tell her the liquidiser was broken. I meekly asked for a sieve; I could lie no longer. P ran her hands through her hair and then sat down to think about what had to be done. The telephone rang. "X doesn't know if he can make it and is sending along his girlfriend ahead of him," P said walking back into the room. That made twenty-one. I said, "But do you know X's girlfriend?" "No, I thought *you* did."

7.20. The tables were set and chairs more or less in the appropriate places. A frenzied clean-up went on in the kitchen (it is visible from the dining room). "I really have to feed my dog. Where's a bowl?" "They are all on the table." "Surely there must be another one somewhere!" "*No!*" Nerves were getting frayed. P disappeared. I fed the spaniel while he struggled to stand still amidst all these new smells. He would be banished to the study again very soon, and very sadly. The cats gingerly crept in, took one look, and flew out. P reappeared with twenty-three crisply ironed napkins. "Where did you get these?" "I just ironed them." I was about to drop. It was ten minutes to eight.

"We've got at least half an hour. No one will come before eight-twenty, especially in this rain." As the last syllable fell, the doorbell rang. No, it couldn't be. It was.

I dashed out of the kitchen, grabbing a bottle of champagne and two glasses and hid in the conservatory. P knew where to find me. The bottle was emptying fast, and I was no less exhausted. I did some sums to divert my mind. Five bottles of champagne could never stretch to twenty-odd people even if we were careful and stingy. There was no whisky or gin or vodka in the house. India. P had to be found. I reeled off the awful statistics. "Orange juice," she said calmly. Somehow they were squeezed. The bottles stretched. I was drunk.

Most of the people were very late. I was getting drunker, swilling the non-arrivals' aperitifs, without orange juice. Then X showed up before his girlfriend and Y appeared with two extra people whom neither P nor I knew. The placement was clearly going to be wrong. The dog barked furiously in the study. P disappeared, chairs were shuffled, soup cups and spoons were miraculously found. P and I (weaving noticeably) led our guests into dinner.

Dinner. Finally. It was an unqualified failure. The tomato consommé was very liquid. "What a lovely colour of red this soup is," several people murmured. The tomato-haters looked out the black windows. "Is it supposed to be quite so runny?" the more inquisitive asked. P and I looked wistfully out the windows. Then the gnocchi. The gnocchi. I never want to hear that word again. It browned beautifully in the oven. P smiled. I sighed. She handed me the first of two pans. I carried it gently to the marble slab, readjusted the oven-cloth and went back for the second. My readjustment had been too radical. My thumb seared with pain. I gritted my teeth and dashed to put it down. My dash had been too radical. The precious tomato sauce leapt across the entire kitchen floor. None was left in the saucepan. The diners laughed. P rolled her eyes. I sobered, quickly. The tomato-haters had little sympathy.

Dessert. The coffee granita had frozen rock-solid. We had forgotten to fork it for the past two hours. We all had more to drink. The gooseberry ice was a surprise – it had not failed. Then a spaniel came exploding through the dining room door, rushed into the kitchen, encountered three cats peacefully nibbling at all the leftover gnocchi, executed an abrupt about-face, and sped back into the dining room. He bit the first exposed calf. There was a loud scream. The cats were now in hot pursuit. Bottles toppled from the table. I ran after the frightened spaniel, tripped, knocked wine out of several glasses. P covered her eyes. Those who were not laughing raced to the door. There was a great deal of barking and skidding across the floor. It was not straightforward pandemonium.

No one would give me a lift back to Montagu Square.

We have not had a dinner party for months.

By the time Stanley celebrated his second London anniversary, in the summer of 1971, his pleasant surprise at having survived the first year had given way to a fierce determination to remain permanently. Englishness fit him like a glove.

Already he had the accent right. Professor Higgins may have heard something off-center in the vowel sounds, but less fanatical ears heard them as English, not foreign, sounds – maybe those of an Englishman who had lived for a while in America; new acquaintances rarely suspected that his origins were American.[10] British usage, spelling and punctuation came to him by now as naturally as the American versions had ever done.

He was pleased to learn that he had an instinctive affinity for English irony, and an uncanny sense of how to be amusing (and amused) in an English way. And the subtlety and reserve of the English felt comfortable, more suited to his temperament than the effusiveness and overintimate manners of Americans.

Clearly, London was a place where he could be challenged intellectually and yet preserve his emotional privacy; no one would probe his American past if his English presence were sufficiently compelling, especially if he demurred when asked about it. There was room here for someone who was slightly eccentric, so long as he was basically correct, and he knew that mastery of English "correctness" would come with continued observation and study. The remaining rough American edges

would be smoothed over in time, as he gained more expo-
sure, as his circle of friends and opportunities for experience
expanded.

⌣⌐⌣

If Stanley were to single out the most significant day, the
one on which his London life was truly launched, he would
surely select the day in October 1971 when he climbed the
stairs to a small Belgravia flat – filled with Bloomsbury art
and books and memorabilia – and met Frances Partridge. He
had come on an academic errand, to enquire about her late
husband, Ralph, who had worked with Leonard and Virginia
Woolf at the Hogarth Press in the '20s; he left having made
in her one of the dearest friends of his life.

Though by this point in his thesis work he was "well
and truly sick of Bloomsbury (what a delight it must be
to wake up and not have to think of them – the Woolfs),"
he couldn't help but feel a revivified interest when he met
Frances. Born in 1900, she was a child of the Edwardian era,
Stanley's favorite period, the one he adopted for himself. As
a very young girl she had known his idol, Henry James, and
then had a Strachey (Julia) for best friend and schoolmate.
As a young woman she had known most of the writers and
artists of Bloomsbury: her sister had married David Garnett
who later married Angelica, daughter of painters Vanessa
Bell and Duncan Grant, and niece of Virginia Woolf; her
own liaison with Ralph Partridge had disrupted the fragile
ménage he maintained with Dora Carrington and Lytton
Strachey. And now she had blood-ties and close friendships
with the succeeding generations; her widowed daughter-in-
law, Henrietta, was a Garnett. In sum, she was at the center
of that swirling crosscurrent of books and life and imagination
and reality where Stanley so loved to be.

But Frances neither lived in the past nor sentimentalized
it. Writer, editor, translator, amateur botanist and musician,

pacifist with left-wing political sympathies, Frances in her seventies was at least as vital as Stanley in his twenties. They took to each other immediately. "Her humour, and the originality of her mind, its quickness & deftness, is remarkable and a marvel to witness. And speak of brute will power and strength of character – she's got it all," he wrote in his diary. In hers, Frances wrote: "It seems odd, in view of the huge difference in our ages, but I now feel he's one of my greatest friends. He loves thinking; that's everything."[11]

Soon after their first encounter, they were meeting at least once a week – to dine, go to parties or the cinema, listen to music, discuss books, enjoy conversation. She appreciated his liveliness and originality – "He's so funny, kind, spontaneous *and* intelligent, and has a lovely way of doing his own back-seat talking"[12] – as well as his delicacy and sensitivity – "The extreme tenderness of his feelings might be expressed in floods of tears either at a performance of *Parsifal* or on hearing the sorrows of his taxi driver."[13]

She helped him with all his important writing, from the Hogarth Press thesis to the Sargent biography, and tore her hair on occasion, as did every editor, while attempting to unravel passages of astonishingly tangled prose. She gloried in the pages that worked, and bucked up his writing spirits always. Having recently lost her only child, Burgo, aged twenty-eight, she asked Stanley to be her literary executor, knowing that he would take a son's care with her words.

Stanley was lucky with older women, important women. On one side of the Atlantic was Millicent Bell who had stimulated his intellect and spurred him toward England and a life in literature; on the other side was Frances Partridge, ready to welcome and move him along once he got there. Her rich web of friendships was put at his disposal, and through her he came to love and be loved by a group of warm, erudite, creative people who played a large part in the fulfillment of his social and professional life. They watched "with dazzled wonder" as his English character took firm shape, as he came to embody ever more distinctively a type of gentleman more English than the English, and more lovable and interesting besides.

On the eve of Stanley's departure for a Wagner pilgrimage, Frances wrote in her diary: "He's off to Bayreuth with 8 boiled shirts because his hotel has no valet service and one must wear tails for first-nights. I asked if he would know anyone there. 'No, not actually, but there'll be lots of people like me.' F: 'Stanley, don't you realize that the whole point of you is that none such exists?' "

ARRIVAL

According to all the signs, I have arrived: I have had calling cards printed. Sublimely understated – one needs a magnifying glass to read my address and I was sensible enough not to have a profession printed.

Stanley to Arlene, 1973

A singularly old-fashioned and eccentric way for a young man of the Beatles generation to announce his presence on the scene. Extravagant, too. And in every way characteristic of Stanley – even to the "practical" uses he could make of the cards: impressing shopkeepers who might then open accounts for him, amusing and attracting attention from people he wanted as friends, and, above all, boosting his own morale. His name and address in elegant type on rich stock looked reassuringly substantial.

The address was 1E Montagu Mews North, formerly a coachman's quarters, near Baker Street and Regent's Park. As understated as the cards, it was "a lovely small flat – perhaps first cousins to a tea-cup. I may get claustrophobia, but this part of town is eminently suitable."

It suited him for the rest of his life. "I have never lived so well except when I lived at home. *This* is a home and psychologically I feel at home here," he wrote to his sister in the spring of 1972, after settling in. A few years later, the teacup got a saucer: he rented the ground-floor room directly under his flat and made it into an office. Montagu Mews was now workplace and living space, the hub of his existence.

Worried about his parents' certain reluctance to establish

him in permanent digs while he was still a student without a plan to earn his keep, Stanley was shamelessly manipulative in his letter requesting funds to make the move:

> I really am in two minds about asking you for the favour. To be perfectly selfish, I cannot wait to live alone and yet material considerations naturally dictate otherwise. If all else fails I will move back into one room . . . I hope you are not angry about my asking. In some ways I feel quite bad about it, but by the mere fact that I asked there is no extrication [sic!] whatsoever.

He hauled out every impressive-sounding (if poorly compensated) future prospect he could muster: a book review to be published in the [London] *Times*, the likelihood of getting more writing assignments since he now had a literary agent working on his behalf, and the possibility of part-time employment with the Leonard Woolf estate, sorting through papers, "including many of Virginia's, which makes the job an absolute plum, as I will have a say on what is published [in the Quentin Bell biography]. Arlene will know how important this post is."

His parents came through with money for the lease, minor remodeling, and some basic furnishings. Stanley breathed a sigh of relief and went shopping. His dining-room budget called for inexpensive wicker furniture, but he couldn't resist "a Victorian oval table . . . fiendishly expensive." He just "happened on" a splendid old rug. "I bought a new wing-backed chair that looks like some enormous dry-docked ship, but oh, so comfortable." And so it went with nearly every purchase – one extravagance led to another. The new flat offered endless opportunities for the exercise of good taste, few of which fell within the parameters of a student allowance.

Over the next fourteen years, as Stanley's preferences changed and his income expanded, he tailored his surroundings till they fit him like a custom-made suit – public rooms cozily elegant, warm; bedroom elegantly simple, almost monastic. By the time *The World of Interiors* magazine featured him and his apartment, in 1984, man and milieu shone forth as striking originals.

From the very beginning, Stanley eschewed the advice of design professionals, whose stock in trade he felt was "fuss fuss fuss fuss – and festoon blinds";[1] he preferred to make his own mistakes. With a sensationalism left over from his Boston days of black-painted rooms, he at first painted the narrow entry hall Chinese-lacquer red "which came out like a starlet's lipstick," and then called upon friend Sarah Janson, an architectural *trompe l'oeil* painter, to make it respectable. Eventually, soft gray *faux* marble panels covered the hall and sitting-room walls, while lightly-brushed white clouds floated on the ceiling. Plump armchairs with gray-striped mattress-ticking covers sat comfortably beside a slim French gilded sofa in gray moiré, catching the glow from gas-fired coals in the marble fireplace.

Paintings by friends – Angelica Garnett, Janetta Parladé, Susannah Phillips, among others – hung frame-to-frame in the jewel of a dining room, illuminated by day from a tiny skylight, and at night by a crystal chandelier whose prisms dispersed rainbows of color onto damask napery, silver plate, and dark blue-green walls. From the tiny kitchen he brought forth meals that provoked no less a connoisseur than Sybille Bedford to write: "Your hospitality is so dazzling, your sequence of courses so splendid that one has to forgo the joy of re-telling it to lesser mortals."*

The atmospheric office – a mellow Edwardian cavern with book-lined walls, and lamps that cast a burnished light on desk and sofa, photographs and Sargent prints – adjoined

---

*Happily, in her novels, essays and biography of Aldous Huxley, Sybille Bedford has *not* forborne from telling us about the joy of good food and wine, which she has experienced from a very tender age throughout a long, much-traveled lifetime.

the courtyard which, though shared by other residential and commercial tenants in the mews, bore Stanley's hallmark: white flowers – roses, daffodils, jasmine – which he planted in tubs and tended devotedly.

Though all of this took years of effort to accomplish, Stanley's most beloved possession was acquired quite by accident, early in his householding career, when he returned from a shopping trip with a great deal more (and less) than he had bargained for:

> He had seen a very grand desk he could ill afford but desperately wanted, and arranged with the antiques dealer to make payments of five pounds a week until the fifty-pound price had been met. When after nine weeks the great day dawned, he walked into the shop to collect his purchase. Tied to the leg of the desk was a spaniel puppy, and his heart went out to it. The man said, "Well, actually I'm offering him for sale and he costs fifty pounds." Stanley forfeited the desk for the dog, who turned out to be "a good investment," he claimed, because when he had grown to his full beauty he had a short but very lucrative career on television, as an advertising dog for a tobacco firm. He sat at the feet of a pipe-smoking gentleman while Stanley hollered orders for him to be still for the camera. He was such a success that when he came of age (in dog years), the television company gave him a birthday party at the Ritz – where normally no dogs are allowed – and he was the guest of honour. There were special dog biscuits for him, and cocktails for his master's friends.[2]

And so was launched a long-term domestic relationship of exceptional mutual satisfaction and compatibility. With not a trace remaining of his childhood fear of dogs, Stanley lavished on spaniel Wuzzo (a corruption of "Oiseau") a measure of attention, tenderness and indulgence usually reserved for a much-loved human. And Wuzzo – a true beauty, with champagne-colored curls, floppy silken ears and soulful eyes – in turn provided Stanley with daily companionship and a good excuse (what he called "canine tyranny") for frequent *divertissements* from work – walks, shampoos, pedicures, vet appointments. There were stints at obedience school, too, though the undisciplined ex-Culver cadet made a predictably poor drill sergeant, and Wuzzo was temperamental, balky, and bit people – including Stanley on occasion. Cute and cuddly-looking ("like a bundle of walking laundry"), he deceived most first-time acquaintances, though he was known to people in the mews as "an impossible dog."

Stanley took Wuzzo everywhere, on foot or in the custom-made dickey-seat attached to his sole means of wheeled transportation, a bizarre "safety" tricycle of the sort that enjoyed brief favor among society gents in the 1890s. Stanley looked upon the trike as another of his bargains, since it was less expensive than a car (though ten times more dear than a regular bicycle). He and Wuzzo ordered the rig from Harrods, after this brief exchange:

Doorman: I'm sorry, sir, you can't bring the dog into the store.
Stanley: But it's the dog who is the customer. I am merely accompanying him.
Doorman: In that case, sir, please go through.[3]

The two were inseparable not only in the streets and shops, but in the minds of friends; Stanley's correspondents nearly always sent "love to Wuzzo" in their letters to his master. When Gill Coleridge left the Hogarth Press to begin her career as a literary agent and was asked whom she represented, she replied: " 'One man and his dog.' You couldn't represent Stanley without representing Wuzzo."[4] (And, she adds, only someone with Stanley's genius for meeting exceptional people would have turned up "a gloriously charming veterinarian-writer," who also became her client – as did, eventually, Frances Partridge, Robert Kee, and the Duchess of Devonshire, all of whom were introduced to her by Stanley.)

When after a dozen years Stanley lost the company of Wuzzo, he gained the distinction of owning the only non-Royal dog in England to have an obituary in the London papers:

In the acknowledgments to his masterful new book on Royal portraitist John Singer Sargent, Stanley Olson thanks "the late Professor W. Olson". This is not – as you might think – a relation, but his dog Wuzzo, who after his 12-year diet of steak, delivered by top butchers Allen's, has died of stomach cancer. "It's appropriate," says Olson, "since the only thing he ever thought about was his stomach." A red spaniel, Wuzzo was meant to be christened Oiseau, until Olson was amused by a vet receptionist's phonetic spelling. He was dignified with his academic qualification "because he looked so incredibly sage" – and he helped in Olson's labour of the last five years. "I would read to him, and when he fell asleep, I knew it was boring." In return, he was ferried about in the back of Olson's specially-built tricycle/dog carriage and lived a life of luxury: a bed made at Heals, a rug from the White House, Asprey and Tiffany collar tags, and a table at the Ritz (until they banned dogs). Wuzzo's place has now been taken by another spaniel, Ambrose. However, he has left his mark. In Fulham, there is a caterers called Wuzzo Foods ("He was their best client"). His ashes are to be buried beneath a sapling in Hyde Park ("Since he watered every tree there"). And Angela Conner, sculptor of the Yalta monument, has completed a bronze bust of him. It's a dog's death.[5]

"I had some wretched news from the bank yesterday," a free-spending Stanley wrote to his sister in the summer of 1972. "I am £200 overdrawn. This moving has devastated me. I also owe money left and right, but I am not too worried – like hell I am not. I am on a ruthless budget to match my diet and I hope to suffer from diminuendo on two fronts."

When he saw his own name included among the worthies

acknowledged by Quentin Bell in the second volume of the Virginia Woolf biography, he wrote Arlene: "I told you I would back into fame." The more likely route, however, was "via Newgate Prison" as a debtor: "I will be detained for Her Majesty's pleasure before the day is out, I am certain."

A visit from his parents brought an end to his money worries for the time being. "I am reaping in the glories of parental attentions: a new typing machine, a marvellous leather sofa, and a new gramophone as well as my overdraft being crossed by the fierce pen of SLO. Mighty is the cheque-book and long may it reign." But no sooner had his father bailed him out of one financial scrape than he got himself into another: "I suppose my holiday in Copenhagen will be courtesy of Lloyd's Bank. Of course Lloyd's don't know it yet and I will not tell them . . ."

Back in Miami, where his parents and Arlene had now settled permanently (Norman lived in California), there were endless family discussions – almost a Scheme-of-the-Month plan – about how best to handle Stanley's profligacy with money, his perpetual overdrafts and ballooning charge accounts. None of their arrangements worked. When they paid him an allowance, he regularly overspent it; when a trust fund replaced the allowance, he overspent that. His brother felt their father was too lenient; his mother said there was little point in fussing so much when they would just have to pay anyway; his sister warned him when tempers were short, and warned the others when Stanley was about to arrive in Florida hat in hand.

He dreaded these visits. He hated Florida (had a lifelong aversion to heat and vulgarity, both of which Miami had in abundance), and hated asking for money. He got so nervous beforehand, "my fingernails look like the battlefields of the 1st World War; next week they will move into the bombsite region." But his need was great, his persistence formidable, and in the end his debts were covered, usually with a check generous enough to start him down the road to more spending trouble. ("Schemes are progressing for [a trip to] Russe. I will read *War and Peace* on the train there, *Anna Karenina* between St Petersburg and Moscow, and Turgenev on the way to London via Wien.")

He was beginning to think of making a career as a writer, he told Arlene: "Academia becomes less and less attractive daily, so if things turn out alright on the writing side of it I may not have to cow-tow [sic] to absurd Universityism." Literary journalism appealed far more: "Book reviewing is no light matter; it is hellishly time consuming and draining. But there is a great reward when I roll out of bed and see my name in print even if I want to hide from everyone I know out of sheer fright of what they will say. I have been extremely lucky."

Arlene, on the other hand, was knee-deep in academia, doing her art history graduate work in a most unhelpful environment. He didn't envy her:

> Miami for a start is the stranglehold of intelligence. One goes against the stream if one has it. The "helpful hens" would not know an original thought if it knocked them down in the street, or stole the playing cards from their hands. Books? What are they? Something to hold up the wall or use for dust-traps? No, I don't think I could bear it, so you in your own way must rise above it – and heaven knows you don't have far to go in Miami to rise above it.

When she got writer's block at thesis time, her sagacious little brother (who had already put in over three years on his own thesis) responded in a tone his English friends would come to know well, an endearingly preachy blend of compassion and firmness:

> After reading your depressed letter I felt that I was listening to my own voice. This business with work can only be seen as essential. In a way it is like childbirth. You live with the

material day in and day out; get sick; get migraines; want to chuck it in – and yet it is what you love. When of course the carrying gets to be too much you give birth to your work and then you wonder what all the fuss was about: it seems so clear. It is essential to worry. It is a sign that you not only care but that the end product will be that much better for all your concern. I am not going to say don't worry, for that will corrupt my theory; worry is an essential offshoot of mental activity. Now depression is a different matter. You must not let it devolve to that plane.

Clearly he knew the difficulties inherent in creative work; less clear was whether and how he expected to support himself doing it. He veered from scenarios of someday achieving fame and wealth through his writing (these large-ly for export to Miami) to more realistic statements made to Arlene: "Admittedly, writing is a career determined to leave me hard-up all my life . . ." Anyhow, he developed a serviceable rationale for accepting long-term financial aid from his parents (though he got rather testy when Arlene called a spade a spade):

I would appreciate it if you would not mention "Fam-ily Welfare," simply because I do not like (or need) the reminder . . . After all I NEVER forget it; I never will, and yet the freedom of it is so great that I do not see fit to expend any energy thinking about it; I try merely to get the most value for money. It resolves itself to an energy thing: worry takes twice as much effort as work, so each hour you spend worrying you have taken two from your work. Which is more important? . . . My role is to demonstrate firstly to myself that F[amily] W[elfare] is a viable investment, and my work must show it; and secondly, if I am convinced, Mir and Sid will fall into thinking the same. I am dedicating my book [thesis] to them, not for the financial investment, but the faith which they have demonstrated through money . . . the one most valuable means at their command.

No matter the gloss he put upon it, at bottom he felt entitled: his parents had money; he needed money; they should give him money. If they couldn't think of it as an investment, they might perhaps consider it philanthropy – a contribution to "a larger good," like supporting the arts, for he would use it to live artfully while doing work he loved. Besides, if he had expensive taste, it was a trait he had inherited from them; he didn't bear full responsibility for his extravagant nature. And deep down he had a thrifty streak, to wit: when forced to take a taxi because the bus didn't arrive, he demanded in writing that London Transport reimburse his fare; he tried to save on income taxes by ensuring that expenses exceeded income (wouldn't that reduce the tax bill? he asked his accountant, or even entitle him to a refund?);[6] and he never wasted money buying goods and services of less than the very highest quality – that would be pennywise and pound foolish.

One of his favorite high-quality goods assumed such obsessive importance in 1973 that the entire nation learned of it through the good offices of "PHS," the *Times* Diarist:

(23 October) DEMANDING. Stanley Olson is a frustrated man, given to visiting obscure cake shops and complaining bitterly to friends about the iniquities of life in Modern London. Why? Fortnum and Mason no longer sell chocolate meringues, that is why. And Olson is a chocolate meringue addict. His frustrations became so acute last weekend that friends said to him: "Oh go on with you. If it is that important phone The Times Diary."

Which is why he did, yesterday. He said Fortnum's chocolate meringues were superb: extremely good and very small. But it is not the only shop to have stopped making chocolate meringues. "You can't get them anywhere in London", he said. "Not even at Floris. And my local cake shop, Sagne's, in Marylebone High Street, stopped making them eight months ago. I've been going to Sagne's every week since then beseeching them to make more."

He has also been bashing the ears of the bakery staff at Fortnum's. They tell him that there is no demand for the chocolate meringues. Floris says the same. He says: "Nonsense. I'll offer to buy £10-worth. I demand to know what you mean by 'no demand'." Can anybody help Stanley Olson?

(24 October) CAN DO. I have good news for Stanley Olson whose plight I revealed yesterday. Chocolate meringues can be obtained in London and in the home counties, as readers have been quick to point out. Stanley Comras, a partner in Sagne's, Olson's local cake shop, told me: "I'll make them for him if he asks me." Another reader phoned suggesting that the Gloriette bakery of Kensington made them. In fact, Gloriette generally makes white meringues dipped in chocolate – not the same thing – but will make real chocolate meringues to order.

Mary Couper, of Chislehurst, Kent, phoned and said she would make chocolate meringues for Olson. She added that she would not charge him if he found that they were not up to the standards set by Fortnum and Mason.

Following up another tip, I spoke to Rupert Heron, a baker of Penshurst, Kent. He said he had not made chocolate meringues for 10 to 15 years but would make them if asked. "I think I can dig up the old recipe", he said.

(25 October) RECIPE CORNER. If, even after my chocolate meringue guide yesterday, you still cannot track them down, make them yourself. Nancy Grey, of Kensington, tells me nothing could be easier. "You powder some chocolate", she says, "and mix it with castor sugar. You add the mixture to beaten egg whites and then place dollops of meringue in an oven at minimum heat. Leave for 1½ to 2 hours."

A public relations woman phoned me yesterday to say that Joan Hunter, caterer to Lord De L'Isle, was making me some chocolate meringues. They will be delivered to my office today by Lord De L'Isle's chauffeur.

This was by no means the end of the story, the sweet details of which Stanley recalled in 1980:

REMEMBRANCE OF MERINGUES PAST[7]

I should never have decided to walk that hot afternoon so many summers ago; it was a mistaken concession to my dog. London in the summer is only deceptively pleasant. By the time I reached Piccadilly my mood had completely collapsed. The Burlington Arcade housed no unexpected surprises; if I went into Sackville Street to buy a book, I would only have to carry it home. There remained Messrs. Fortnum & Mason.

We went in, walking in none-too-deliberate haste past the caviar, foie gras and truffles, through to the glacé and preserved fruits, beyond the tins of biscuits and up the dozen or so stairs to the cakes and chocolates on the mezzanine. The sales assistants were wonderfully starched. I gazed and my dog sniffed – it was a pleasure for us both. Then at the end of the silver bakery counter, I saw something I had never seen before: chocolate meringues – not, it must be confessed, objects which entertained the eyes quite as well as they amused the stomach. As examples of the confectioner's art, they were not pretty – merely small, brownish lumps. They were very light, so one got a great many in a quarter of a pound. Yes, I would buy some.

This took place some ten years ago, you understand, and my 3s. 6d. worth weighed nothing. They were lovingly wrapped in that wonderful lightly waxed paper remembered from the bakeries of my childhood, and tied up with red and gilt ribbon round the stiff cardboard box, heavily encrusted with Messrs. Fortnum & Mason's name. It was a very satisfying object.

I walked up Regent Street refreshed and happy, and determined not to walk home. I got a seat on the top of the bus, in the front. London lay stretched out before me, and my meringues beside me. Then temptation overruled etiquette. With a singular lack of delicacy, I tore open the box and ate one, while my dog looked on with a great sense of expectation that led as quickly to dejection. It was a moment

I can scarcely forget. A dissolving more than delicious, the first heady moment of pleasure that was to lead to a strenuous habit.

My visits to Messrs. Fortnum & Mason soon became a weekly ritual. It never occurred to me that they might be delivered. The pattern remained splendidly unvaried, and every time I got off the bus at my flat, about a mile away, all I had to show was a box satisfactorily rifled of its contents. They simply never lasted the distance; any magician would have been proud of me.

This odd behaviour lasted for years. Then it swiftly turned into a nightmare. Imagine my horror when one day I mounted the mezzanine stairs and found an empty tray where my meringues resided. They must have sold out, I told myself. I would have to come back on Saturday morning, which was, of course, a bore, but that could not be helped. It was prudent, however, to take the precaution of asking when they would be making a reappearance.

'I am afraid, sir, that they will not be available on Saturday.'

Of course, the weekend and perishables, I thought – nothing amiss here.

'On Monday, then?' A tone of urgency had crept in; I sensed doom tumbling my way.

'I am sorry, sir. We no longer make them.'

Those were the very words, falling heavily and grimly and intractably – I can hear them still. They tolled the death sentence of one of my greatest pleasures.

'There is no demand for them, sir.' An addendum not only gratuitous but downright incorrect, since I was standing there demanding them. To no avail.

All the way home I muttered to myself various stern and rallying phrases. Hardly an earth-shattering blow, I said; scarcely a profound disruption of one's existence. It had no effect. The removal of chocolate meringues seriously altered the routine of my life.

Meek resignation lasted about a fortnight. It was simply

no good: I *had* to have a chocolate meringue. London was combed as it had never been combed for any confection. The answer was steady, unvarying: 'We haven't made them for years. Can't remember when we last had a call for them. Does anyone eat chocolate meringues these days?' they asked, unhelpfully. 'Why not try Fortnum's?'

I had a vision of myself ending my days with just their tantalising memory. I could see my diary divided between post- and pre-meringue. Weary confectioners tried to fob me off with chocolate-covered meringues. The search was going from bad to worse. My complaints were extreme, and I was beginning to bore even myself. Friends were avoiding me.

Then, a brainwave: The *Times* Diary was the place to complain. The diarist ran the story of my search. Laughter was heard across England and, when it subsided, a more practical response was heard. Recipes flowed in, controversy was born. Did one use cocoa powder or shredded chocolate in the egg whites? What proportion of sugar to cocoa? What size? Should one sprinkle or stir? It was very serious stuff.

The bakers of Britain rose to my aid. Country ladies rang me up. Would I sample their efforts? Would I! I got invitations to tea every day for a month. Kind chefs sent me box after box. Vanloads were delivered to The *Times*' offices and swiftly sent on to me. One day I was the proud recipient of twenty-five dozen chocolate meringues. And the deluge had just begun. It was a bad joke to me, and heaven for my dog. Every breath he took was perfumed with the exciting smell of chocolate, and it must be noted that spaniels and chocolate are very happy partners. It gave me a sick headache and crept into every room. Waking up to the smell of chocolate is not to be recommended.

I gave chocolate meringue parties. My dinner menus featured them for weeks. Waking or sleeping, my mind, my sight, was filled with them. It was clearly a case of famine or feast, and the feast showed no sign of coming to an end. The *Times* diarist confessed with a sigh that he wished he had never heard of me or chocolate meringues. He seemed to be a modern version of the Sorcerer's Apprentice, conjuring out of the air ever-higher mountains of meringues. As a final desperate measure, he printed a tried and approved (by me) recipe. The best of all sent to him was the simplest: 'Powder some chocolate, mix it with sugar and add the mixture to the beaten egg whites, then place dollops (about 4 inches round) in the oven at minimum heat for 1½ to 2 hours.'

The great chocolate meringue controversy that gripped England in October 1973 came to a fitting conclusion. One afternoon a huge Rolls-Royce limousine sailed majestically up to my front door. The impeccably liveried chauffeur got out and delivered into my hands one dozen equally impeccable meringues, each wrapped in pink tissue and accompanied by a substantial basin of Devon cream and a vast monogrammed damask table-napkin. A peer of the realm's chef had smiled on me. And yet ... somehow it was not quite the same as that weekly bus-ride back from Messrs. Fortnum & Mason.

"Bloomsbury was saved from arrogance by its capacity to laugh at itself, by the irony with which it regarded its own activities as well as those of others, and by its joy in absurdity, wherever encountered."[8] So, too, with Stanley. This saving grace was as evident in his letters – especially the long, newsy ones to old friends far away and long out of touch – as in his conversation. The deflating self-mockery, the "back-seat commentary" on his own words, the ironic humor and wit – so vividly, unmistakably his and no one else's – made reading a letter from Stanley nearly as delightful an experience as talking with him in person:

[To Phyllis – November 26, 1973]
Today seems to be the one that has been selected, quite inadvertently, to catch up on wildly overdue communications

to the past. But indeed it is not the past, rather an attempt to bridge the great void of silence. First Sam [a college friend] rang me absolutely out of the blue from Boston. Then your father rang me on his whirlwind London tour. Now insomnia, an appallingly regular feature of my life these days, has prompted me to write to you. Mind you, my memory was substantially jogged yesterday when I made my bookings to go to San Francisco to discharge familial duty there, and was told that a flight stopped in Seattle. I would very much like to see you if you are in that part of the world in late December. I will ring you, in any case. A voice, and especially yours, would be a delight to my ears.

I see that insomniac gush has penetrated this letter already, despite efforts to the reverse. So I will retreat to giving you news – whatever *that* is. The fabled PhD degree is done, in fact was done last January, and with it Bloomsbury. It is quite overdone now. McKay Publishers have asked me to do a biography of Elinor Wylie and I will begin it in January after I sign the contract.[9] She is a sublime subject: short life, packed with incident, a distinguished battery of lovers and husbands, nymphomania, beauty, and if that isn't enough, talent – though of the most bizarre sort. I am quite excited about it, I don't mind confessing. I am also publishing book reviews in the Times and doing a substantial amount of journalism. In short, I am suffering from that most delightful thing called success and happiness. I seem to have no complaints – no personal ones, that is, but like the Sitwells, one has to complain about rank stupidity, greed, and arrogance that, like some trinity plague, have swept the world. It is a losing battle at the best of times, and ulcer-giving all the time.

But to more pleasant things: music. Wagner is still in the forefront. I hope to see the Metropolitan Opera's Tristan in January. And Bayreuth is doing 8 Tristans this summer and I will be there for two and one Ring. (If the tickets come through, would you like to come? July 25th till whenever you feel you've had enough?) Thank god there is no Parsifal this year to clog the festival. I recently – in fact, minutes ago – listened to Porgy and Bess, which is divine. I do wish it would be staged again. Such glorious music and a story that could wrench even the most philistine of hearts.

As I remember, when I spoke to you last, some 2 years ago, you were being baptised by Virginia Woolf. Any conclusions? Last week I played a game called Desert Island Books, selecting 10 books to accompany one on a desert island, logically enough. Mine were, and I see this is by no means a subtle way to recommend books, among others: Goethe's *Elective Affinities*, Stendhal's *The Red and the Black*, Michael Holroyd's biography of Lytton Strachey, Ford's *The Good Soldier*, Bennett's *The Old Wives' Tale*, James' *The Golden Bowl* . . . but this is too pompous for even me to continue with, especially as you probably know them all already. What I have read recently – no, I think devoured would be a more accurate word – is E F Benson's Mapp and Lucia series, some 7 novels, all of which are sublimely trivial and elegantly written.

Really, I think this self-indulgence is unforgivable and embarrassing. But after two years of silence, what does one say? Sinking in the well of the first-person pronoun is certainly the worst way. I am unable to be provocative at 3 in the morning; moreover, to write platitudes is beyond me all the time. In short, this wretched account of what is going on in my pea-sized brain is an attempt to let you know that I am well, hope you are, and a bait to lure you into writing. Please forgive the vulgar tone of this letter, and overlook its total want of anything worth replying to.

By the end of 1973 when Stanley acquired his calling cards, it no longer looked as though he'd have to "back into fame" – via debtor's prison, letters to the *Times* Diary, or acknowledgments in other people's books. His prospects appeared promising indeed: he had a flat of his own, a dog for companion, a degree that conferred the title "Dr" (balm to any vestigial Culver wounds and a help in obtaining credit from shops), a growing collection of friends, and, lo and behold, he was about to sign a book contract.

"Turning back now is out of the question judging from my

successes so far," he wrote his parents, by way of emphasizing his decision to remain in London and requesting more money to sustain him there. Like his model and mentor Henry James one hundred years earlier, Stanley believed: "If I keep along here patiently for a certain time I rather think I shall become a (sufficiently) great man."[10]

A PERFECT FIT

*Stanley seemed so English that had he been a Russian spy –
or an American one, for that matter – he would certainly have
fooled me.*

Geoffrey Phillips, solicitor

*He was more of an English gentleman than an English gentle-
man. His accent – even his voice. His ear was impeccable.*

Frances Partridge

He was one of us.

Lady Selina Hastings

No one would have expected Stanley Olson to take the clichéd role of The American Abroad – Burberry raincoat, Savile Row suit, and all the rest of it. But it was a stroke of genius that in selecting, researching, and crafting the character he was to become in London, he strayed so far from the norm, choosing to go back in time, to become an historical anachronism, a cultural artifact, a "type" that no longer existed (may never have existed, really), yet would fascinate and evoke nostalgia in many of the people whose friendship he courted.

His natural affinity with the decades around the turn of the century, supplemented by his scholarship and meticulous attention to detail, gave him an exceptional command of his adopted role. "He got it brilliantly right all the way down the line," says Selina Hastings. "He knew much better than any of us did what was right for that time. It was a great work of art."

He traveled with the oldest Baedeker guides he could

find, shunned most modern contraptions, and recreated in his domestic surroundings the atmosphere of the period he was writing about. Personal life and professional life were all of a piece; he not only researched his biographical subjects' lives, he breathed their air:

> My life is now c. 1910. When the library told me some books I requested, published in 1919, were lost in the bombing, I hastily pointed out that the last Zeppelin raid on London was 1917 so they couldn't fob that off on me. I stood my ground demanding my books, when an essential detail was pronounced: World War II. I had completely forgotten about it. Perhaps one ought to boast about having achieved oblivion – so I refused to be embarrassed.[1]

If anyone only slightly less gifted than Stanley had assumed this persona, the result would have been caricature. "With him it came across as a higher, less common style of doing things."[2] Through sheer force of character and ability, and from a blend of seemingly contradictory qualities – calculation and naturalness – he had forged a new self that grew rapidly to maturity, reached its apogee during his work on the Sargent biography, and prevailed even after his first stroke.

If as a boy he had seemed a cuckoo's egg in the Olson family nest, now as a man amongst his London friends he seemed more like a Fabergé egg – the product of imagination and craftsmanship, a museum piece. Over the course of the London years, "he constructed a style of living which supplied his friends with endless awestruck anecdotes,"[3] and people on both sides of the Atlantic dined out on Stanley-stories.

My own favorite Stanley-story is set in January 1986, when I made my first trip to London. I hadn't seen him since our

Boston years, since his transformation, but I felt comfortable with him immediately. The patina of *belle-époque* grandeur highlighted rather than concealed his old lovable self. I was accustomed to his accent from telephone conversations over the years, and I had kept up with his writing, reading, and musical doings through our correspondence. But I was not fully prepared for the impeccable manners, exquisite taste, and impossibly high standards that now were married to his familiar warmth and wit.

After a long afternoon catching-up session in his flat, he rang for a taxi. We were to dine at Claridge's, he said. I didn't yet know of his special relationship with the place, that it was his second home, his "club." I only knew that it was one of the grandest, most expensive hotels in London, and while I was flattered that he would use the occasion of my visit for such a splurge, I was very uncomfortable about going there. I had expected to walk to some informal neighborhood bistro and was dressed accordingly. He brushed aside my objections – that I looked terrible, that Claridge's was too expensive, that I wouldn't know how to behave in such posh surroundings – and made it clear that his decision was final. He took off his house slippers (lined in red leather), slipped on his shoes (lined in red leather), donned his overcoat (lined in red silk), and we headed downstairs into the courtyard of the mews to await the cab.

I asked him to show me his writing room while we waited. As I stepped into the enchanting book-lined office, there was an outrageous squeal: I had trod upon a "Spitting Image" of Ronald Reagan's head – a rubber squeeze toy loved by Stanley's puppy. I coveted the object and he gave it to me. "He's *your* President," he said, with expatriate smugness. I stuffed it into my bulky travel handbag and we climbed into the taxi. Each time my arm bumped the handbag, Ronnie squealed, loudly, and we giggled as if we were still kids in Akron.

When we arrived at Claridge's Stanley looked troubled.

He noticed unusual outdoor illumination and sensed security precautions. (There had been a rash of Middle East-related terrorist activity and threats, and the mood in London was somewhat tense.) He asked the cabbie to wait while he made inquiries of the doorman. "Sharpshooters on the roof," he said when he returned. "Shimon Peres and other Israeli and British officials are dining here."

"I'm scared," I said. "Let's go someplace else. This is dangerous. Besides, what if they search us and find a Reagan caricature in my pocket? And what if he squeaks? They'll think I'm a security risk and put us out."

"At Claridge's they would *never* search a woman's handbag!" he said, as if that would relieve my anxiety. I wanted them to search everything and everyone. I did not want to go in.

"The worst of it," he said, "is that the staff will be on edge and preoccupied. The food will be off. Service will be lax."

He decided to go for a drink anyway. Once inside he could better assess the mood of the kitchen and the ill effects of this invasion from "the real world, so-called."

He deposited me at the door of what he called the "ladies' cloakroom," which I assumed was a British euphemism for what Americans euphemistically call a "restroom," but which turned out to be a sort of *salon* with beauty rituals and tipping etiquette unfamiliar to me. A uniformed attendant hung my knockabout coat in a mirrored cupboard filled with the other guests' furs, then pointed toward the toilet enclosures and sinks, and then implied, wordlessly, that I should sit down at one of the skirted dressing-tables where I could make use of the cosmetics and hairbrushes laid out for my convenience.

I emerged from this intimidating adventure to find Stanley seated on a silk-upholstered sofa at a small gilt cocktail table. A hawk-eyed muscle-bound bodyguard-type was trying to be inconspicuous on an Empire chair across the room, and a footman in eighteenth-century livery was taking Stanley's drink order. The bodyguard looked straight at me as I took my seat beside my host; Ronnie had made an obscene noise when I clutched my handbag to my side.

The manager came over to greet Stanley, who introduced me as "Mrs Hatfield," a title I had neither used nor heard in many years. He said the state dinner was nearly over, the dining room would be restored to calm, and Mr Olson would soon find everything to his satisfaction. The seated bodyguard hoicked himself and his Empire chair a few feet to the right, to survey the room from a different angle.

Well into my second drink and feeling like Alice in a Looking-Glass world where everyone was at ease except me and the bodyguards, I treated my host to a critical commentary: on the rigid decorum of the place, the theatrical footmen, the blue-haired dowagers under surveillance as they sipped their cocktails, the anachronistic form of his introduction. Stanley seemed tickled by all of my observations up to the last, on which point he was not amused and began to scold: "Mrs" is polite, correct; the staff could hardly address me by my first name, after all, and it would be unkind to put them in the position of having to guess whether I was "Miss," "Mrs" or "Lady" Hatfield.

I felt this last alternative was far-fetched, to say the least, but his earnestness impressed me. He was genuinely put out, irritated. When I proposed "Ms" as the *au courant* title to cover such uncertainties, and one which I preferred because of its focus on the woman, not her husband or father, he said "Not done here." I spluttered objections for a moment, but then laughed at the drollery of feminist protest in this bastion of the *ancien régime* and lifted my glass to acknowledge his etiquette lesson. Cousin Stanley was instructing me about his chosen world – the Old World, no doubt, but a milieu whose refinements and nuances he had somehow made his own. If I wanted to understand him, I had better listen.

At the time of our dinner at Claridge's (six months before his crippling stroke, as it turned out), Stanley had reached his peak – attained the apotheosis of Sargent-influenced grandeur – though I didn't know that then. There was a lot I didn't yet know. But it was very clear even then, even to me, that Stanley had achieved mastery of a certain kind of English life. And I – who shared his roots, his background, yet was so very different from him – knew how much he'd had to study and learn (about England) and put aside (about America) to become the self-assured gentleman who faced me across the table. It had taken courage to make a commitment to an altogether new life, and I thought him brave to have done so; not affected, but courageous.

Years after that dinner and our tiff about titles, I found among Stanley's papers the draft of an etiquette book which he proposed to be, among other things, "a handy reference to the science of negotiating the complexities of social life, a key to the mysteries of polite behaviour neatly unfolded in example and precept." When I read his disquisition on manners, I gained insight into why we had run afoul of each other that evening. Where Stanley made a clear distinction between manners and morality, I had linked them. From his perspective, "Mrs" is manners not morals, and manners are not to be confounded by politics – especially sexual politics:

Manners balance social intercourse, help us *appear* to be equal. They trace the limits of behaviour, giving everyone a neat area to roam around in, without intimidating anyone else. They rarely draw their strength from honesty – quite the reverse. The activity of manners is not to probe into truth or reflect sincerity, but to overpaint every occasion with a film that covers all irregularities and obscures all extremes of emotion or any other departure from pleasure.

But manners are not a straitjacket on your character; they are a refinement of it. If you behave well you are not denying some ultimate statement your soul is trying to shout out. Church is the place for confession, not the Hunt Ball. Social life is an exploration along the superficial, and there is no point crusading for substance.

Manners form a carapace, a thin carapace that shelters your personal adaptation of standards, your individual version of ideals, your private network of values. Thus, if you were a mollusc you would *look* like every other oyster lining the seabed; yet once your shell was prised open a rare gem might be exposed. If there is no pearl inside, manners help to postpone that disappointment.

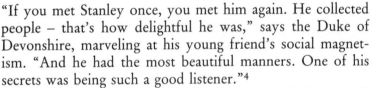

"If you met Stanley once, you met him again. He collected people – that's how delightful he was," says the Duke of Devonshire, marveling at his young friend's social magnetism. "And he had the most beautiful manners. One of his secrets was being such a good listener."[4]

Another was having a well-calibrated sense of what would "do" and what would not do in the various circles in which he moved. Whether he charmed them at stately homes, bullied them in the neighborhood, importuned them at the shops, or dazzled them coming and going, most people found the force of Stanley's personality irresistible; succumbing to his will seemed both pleasant and inevitable. Even negative adjectives – spoiled, naughty, demanding, greedy – when applied to him (as they not infrequently were) lost their sting. People described his "wickedness" in one breath and in the next said "He was *enchanting*! I *adored* him!"

Apparently, manners that were beautiful and "old-fashioned, slightly overdone – eccentric, really" would do quite well indeed.[5] One introduction led to another, friends of friends took him up, and his calendar filled with engagements for lunch, drinks or dinner (often all three) almost every day. There were invitations for weekends and holidays at country houses and palatial homes in England and abroad; even "Her Britannic Majesty's Ambassador" once requested his presence (with Frances Partridge) at an embassy luncheon in Paris. The social whirl ebbed infrequently, and then only when he purposely withdrew – either from physical exhaustion or on account of a reforming impulse – to work, to diet, to abstain from alcohol.

But it would be wrong to imagine Stanley as a social butterfly, flitting from party to party, adding yet another acquaintance to his string. Extroverted though he was, witty and engaging as he could be on first acquaintance, it was in more intimate surroundings and with those he knew well that he truly shone. "He was so devoted," says Kerstin Williams. "You felt you were a recipient of so much love. It was just extraordinary – the quality of his friendship. A sort of love at a distance . . ."[6]

As one who didn't like sex ("food is better," he told a friend) and abjured love affairs (sweeter in his romantic imagination than they could ever be in real life), Stanley instead applied his emotional energy and a huge proportion of his time to friendship, for which he had an exceptional capacity – and an exceptional range: men and women of all ages, some very grand, some down to earth, each made to feel that he or she occupied a special niche in his heart and mind. Women, particularly, found in him – and he in them – a capacity for rich companionship. "It was extraordinary how Stanley, without the advantage of sex appeal, had such intense relationships with such remarkable women," Angelica Garnett says, wondering if sex appeal might not have been rather a hindrance.[7]

When Stanley took to somebody, the amount of care and attention he lavished on the relationship was stunning.

Sue Baring,* with whom he became "instant friends" when Robert Kee† introduced them, recalls:

> Quite soon after I met him, when he was at the peak of his culinary delight, and cooking and doing extraordinary, extravagant dishes – he prepared the most amazing dish of all, a quail inside a grouse inside a pheasant inside a chicken. It was unbelievable! And to start we had a delicious smoked fish. He laid it all out in the dining room, with enormous white damask table napkins, marvellous glasses – we had a beautiful bottle of claret. Then we had an incredible iced soufflé. And it was all just to honour me! We sat there over lunch – just him and me – till about half past four. He'd taken *so* much trouble to give me this feast. And nothing unhappy had happened, and it wasn't my birthday. I think he just wanted to show me how much he liked me – for myself, not just in connection with Robert.

On the other hand, he wasted not a moment trying to charm people who bored or annoyed him. And when he took against people, "they went right into his doghouse and stayed there," says Janetta Parladé, who "remonstrated sometimes about his being monstrously unjust about someone."**

Stanley's brand of charm was not the typically ingratiating sort; he rarely drew on reserves of sweetness and light. Instead he conquered by "his brilliance in conversation, his glorious

---

*The Hon. Susan Baring, OBE, JP; ex-wife of The Hon. John Baring (now Lord Ashburton), magistrate, closely involved in penal reform and human rights. She has a wide circle of friends in the literary and musical life of London.

†Robert Kee was a bomber pilot in World War II, after which he became a writer and journalist. He is the author of fifteen books, including *The Green Flag*, a history of Irish nationalism which has remained in print for twenty-two years. He has worked for the past thirty-five years in BBC radio and television and Independent Television.

**Janetta Parladé divides her time between England and Spain, home of her husband, Jaime. In both countries she is known, not only as a painter, but as an "enchanting" hostess and a "magical" cook. She met Stanley through Frances Partridge, her close friend for over fifty years, and figures prominently in Frances's published diaries.

sense of fun, his dandyism and feeling for quality."[8] He was "sensitively brilliant," says Angelica Garnett.

And he was bold. When an unusual foodshop and delicatessen called Hobbs opened in London in 1981, it was for a while "the meeting point of everybody who wanted good food."[8] Stanley promptly became Hobbs' star customer, upstaging "the grandest, most well-known people" who shopped there, by demanding and receiving more attention than anyone else. He appreciated not only the merchandise on offer but the attractive and clever young staff, including several members of the Williams family – all of whom eventually became his good friends.* Kerstin Williams's encounter with Stanley typifies his often outrageous approach to a new person he found potentially interesting:

I'd never met him before and he just came up to me and said, "Well, Miss Hitler, do you think you look nice in those leather trousers and boots?" I thought he was the rudest, funniest thing I'd ever come across! I had an apron on, but clearly he'd examined what I was wearing underneath and he loved it. He was just teasing, being obnoxious, trying to get one's attention.

Romilly Hobbs [later Lady McAlpine] tried to run this highly sophisticated and elegant shop, with a fine, intelligent staff and impeccable decorum, and Stanley would come in and throw it all open. The organization completely disintegrated. People became silly in his company; they started enjoying themselves and everyone's facade collapsed. And he could be giggly silly, but he had the highest standards and knew exactly what he wanted.

He was unscrupulous about people's time. He got away with murder. He'd have everyone running round. He'd say to me:

---

*Kerstin's husband, cellist Jonathan Williams, and his brother and sister the twins Patrick and Katy Williams are all professionally involved with food or music or both.

"I want this delivered by one-thirty," and it was very, very busy in the shop, but somehow this was allowed. One could go and deliver to him. Then I used to sit there at his flat and talk with him for an hour or two. And because you'd been at Stanley's, everything was forgiven, by Romilly and everybody.

One morning he bought fish and said, "You must bring it round to me because I've got important people coming for lunch." So I did, because I loved talking to him anyway, and then I'd arrive and he'd say: "Well, *you're* an important person. Let's have some lunch!" He used to do that when I least expected it. Or he'd just pop into Hobbs with bunches of violets, because he'd found them on the corner and knew I liked them.

Alongside his more intense relationships, Stanley fancied amusing, quick-witted people who were lively conversationalists and enjoyed gossip – be they rich or poor, aristocrats or shopkeepers, intellectuals or neighbors in the mews; their place in the social hierarchy was less important than their ability (and availability) to distract him from work and self, his moods and emotions. (A young, trendy set he called "The Moderns" met these qualifications for a brief spell; they were "rich, uneducated, never read a book, loved pop music, Jaguars, and hash," he later told a friend.)[9] To be *in* good company, he felt, was to be with people who were not overly preoccupied with themselves; to *be* good company was to avoid "sinking in the well of the first-person pronoun."

But he *was* ambitious, and curious too (in the way of a social outsider and a professional biographer), and the people he most wanted to be with and on whom he set his sights were the aristos – those of the peerage, like the Duke and Duchess of Devonshire, or those of the mind, like Rebecca West, Frances Partridge, Sybille Bedford. In their company his conversation was rich, often deep, and he was always on his best behavior.

Among his familiars in the mews and neighborhood, however, he could behave with a selfishness and arrogance verging on tyranny, as if it were everyone's duty to minister to his needs ("Take me to the plant nursery – now!") and serve his convenience ("Look after Wuzzo this afternoon. G'bye!"). He didn't hesitate to interrupt Ann Dex, whose office was in the mews, whenever he needed a dog-sitter. He especially liked to interrupt when she was on the telephone trying to conduct her artist-management business, since then it would be harder for her to refuse him. "He'd go off for hours and leave Wuzzo. Or the dog would suddenly appear in my office because somebody was hoovering in Stanley's flat. I was trapped and had to cancel all sorts of meetings and appointments because suddenly I had this dog on my hands."[10]

Yet Ann and everyone else always forgave him. Most of his victims knew his bullying was a facade, that if you really stood up to him he'd back off – smile his naughty-boy smile and go away. A few realized that it was an escape valve – that he couldn't behave this way with his grander friends and that he was letting off steam where it was safe. Some took vicarious pleasure in his swell doings – his occasional visits to titled people and stately homes – and he made sure to tell everyone delicious stories when he returned.

Brigit Appleby, a potter and photographer who owned a boutique in the neighborhood, says:

He was the bossiest, most bullying, rudest little man whom I absolutely adored. Because he was so bright, and because he had heart and a wonderful sense of humour, and was so *gentle* under that facade. He never spoke a cliché or had a trite thought, and his smallest of small-talk was fascinating, challenging, rewarding. Being with him was like sunshine and a thunderstorm all at once – very exciting. Because you never knew what he might say that would get you . . .

Around sisterly Ann or motherly Brigit he could let down his guard. "He didn't have to *be* something with us. He didn't have to protect his 'image'; we teased him out of it. And," adds Brigit, "I'm bossier than he is, and he soon realized that."

No one could be more amusing than Stanley in the good times, more encouraging when one's morale faltered, or more sensitive and attentive in times of trouble – and this applied as much to those he occasionally bullied as to those he consistently charmed. He made himself available to friends in London at all hours, and if illness or misfortune overtook them while they were away, he telephoned to Spain or France or wherever they happened to be. "You are the nonpareil of cosseters," a woman wrote from abroad, after a gentle barrage of orchids, truffles and long-distance calls from Stanley had eased the pain of the breakup with her lover. His condolence letters communicated genuine sympathy and moved a widowed friend to "the kind of tears that come from having one's misery acutely recognized." When a visitor suddenly burst into tears at his flat and poured out her frustrations in caring for her cranky old mother, "he listened as if he understood exactly what I was going through. Then when I calmed down a bit he said, 'Come on. Let's play croquet.' And we played croquet right there on his sitting-room carpet."

Just as he usually knew the latest gossip before any of his friends, he was frequently the first to learn of bad news, and he went to great lengths to cushion its impact on those affected. He was the sort of friend who would show up on your doorstep at the crack of dawn – before you might hear the news from anyone else – to tell you that today's tabloids had the details of your private life splashed across their pages. Then he'd distract you with the gift of a jasmine plant so large you wondered how he'd fit it and Wuzzo and himself in the taxi – not to mention where he'd bought it in the pre-dawn hours. The sort of friend who, when needing to convey to you the news of a close friend's sudden death, would cut short your time on tenterhooks by traveling across town to a phone booth only minutes away from your flat before ringing to say, "I've got bad news. May I come right over?" And he had a way of being deeply responsive to one's sorrow while remaining helpfully level-headed and unsentimental. To a friend who shared a tale of lost love and resignation to lifelong solitude, he wrote:

(11 May 86) I really mustn't allow your revelation about your exclusion from intimacy to go unnoticed, though such notice as I am able to give will not be on a personal level. Just count your lucky stars you are not one of those people so made as to be ill when forced to experience solitude; they are the ones ripe for really potent unhappiness. Time and time again I've seen people attach themselves to someone so unsuited for harmony that it is tragic, and all because the fear of being alone was greater than the fear of unhappiness. I would hate to suffer from that. I am sorry you are miserable, but I am beginning to believe one is only really happy in retrospect, in memory. It is an awful thing to want to be happy; such a primitive desire. Content, yes; happy . . . well, that is moonshine.

Despite the disclaimer his "notice" was quite certainly "on a personal level." Years before, he too had nearly attached himself to someone with whom harmony was a most unlikely outcome.

(2 April 77) I've been to and fro the hospital all week like some tennis ball designed for that occupation. A friend of mine fell out of a window and broke everything. To think I wasted vital sleep as a child waiting to grow up, full of excitement. Mind you I thought growing up was simply stuffing your mouth with chocolate – and of course it is.

This glib narration to his sister belies the shock, horror

and pity he felt at Henrietta Partridge's attempted suicide, reactions that were particularly intense because, years before, her great-aunt Virginia Woolf's suicide had held a peculiar fascination for him – darkly romantic. But now this came too close for comfort; Henrietta was his contemporary and close friend – her whole family were his friends. He had just been to the opera with her mother, Angelica; he had daily contact with her mother-in-law, Frances; and Sophie, Henrietta's fourteen-year-old daughter, was a great favorite of his.

Stanley went almost daily to the hospital where Henrietta, who had "broken everything" in the way of bones but whose head and face remained miraculously uninjured, lay for months, an exquisite beauty racked with pain. "He was always bringing little presents that he hoped would distract me," she says. Once he brought a box of Italian amaretti cookies, so that he could set afire the tissue papers they were wrapped in, which have a special knack for soaring quickly aloft, making a poofing sound and then disintegrating into hundreds of tiny, beautiful embers, like a miniature sparkler. "It did delight me," she says. "But I was on oxygen!"[11]

Mischief that would have got anyone else permanently banned from the hospital – if not arrested and charged with reckless endangerment – earned Stanley the indulgent regard of the hospital matrons. "They knew he was just trying to please me and that I always felt better after his visits."

Their frequent visits continued after Henrietta's release from the hospital. "He felt sorry for me," she says. They would lie side by side on his sitting-room floor, listening to opera, or spend hours talking about books and writing. He was struggling with Elinor Wylie, she with writing fiction (her novel *Skeletons in the Closet* came out in 1986). She took him to Charleston, her grandparents' country house to which Bloomsbury figures had often retreated and where her grandfather, Duncan Grant, still lived and painted; here they'd sit on the terrace reading aloud to each other from

Henry James's *Portrait of a Lady*.

In the late autumn of 1977 he proposed marriage. "I was rather surprised," Henrietta says, "but since we were such good friends and always had heaps of fun together – a right pair of scallywags – and were also serious about our work, and because of the fact that he was extremely fond of my daughter, I accepted."[12]

"He wanted an English wife with a good pedigree," she says now, looking back. Hers would have seemed ideal to Stanley: Bloomsbury by birth *and* by marriage. "And he wanted *la belle hôtesse*," a role he could well imagine her in, since she was a notable cook and enjoyed entertaining. What he did *not* want was sex. "We discussed the subject and he said he loathed the act – called it 'slimy.' He wasn't gay," she says. "He told me that he'd 'tried it with the boys' years ago, when he first came to London, but it hurt and he didn't like it. He simply didn't like sex. It's untidy and he was very fastidious. But since he knew that *I* liked it, he thought that should I wish to have lovers, we ought to have separate front doors."[13] (Exquisite tact carried to a mad extreme – just the sort that led him to carry a black hankie to the opera "so as not to distract anybody when he used it to dry his tears," says Henrietta.)

News of the engagement reached very few ears (Stanley told only Frances Partridge and Janetta Parladé). "I knew perfectly well that we had both made a terrible mistake," Henrietta says, "that we couldn't possibly put up with each other. Stanley knew it too, but being such a gentleman he had gone and put himself into a frightful pickle." By the time spring came, they had extricated themselves from his impulsive proposal. They remained friends.

Though Stanley's friends ranged in age from young children (he was godfather to Rose Jackson's son Rollo and Kerstin

Williams's daughter Susanna) to nonagenarians, he had an unusual number who were at least one generation older than him, and he worried about losing the eldest among them. "To fear [my own] death seems to me the most absurd thing imaginable," he wrote, at age twenty-five. "The only unfortunate thing is that I know that my dearest friends will pre-decease me and I don't like the idea of going on without them."

He defied the gravity of such thoughts with frequent outbursts of infantile humor; he could "fall about laughing like a schoolboy," friends say, and take "childish delight in some of the silliest things." "He called me 'Thu Thu,' " says Susannah Phillips. "My childhood nickname was 'Susu' and this was his version, inspired by Bishop Tutu. Sometimes he would ring me up and spend at least two minutes singing into the phone 'Hello, Thu Thu Thu, hello . . . ' Bellyaching laughter. Oh, I miss those giggles."

And when his little goddaughter thrust a water-pistol into his hand one hot summer's afternoon and asked him to play, he could do so with the abandon of one of her peers (even if he did keep his jacket on). "He was lying in the bathroom upstairs, hiding out, shooting water at us down in the garden," her mother says.[14]

In addition to biography-writing triumphs and troubles, Stanley and Selina Hastings shared a love for indulging their childish sides. "Often we just relapsed into childhood," she says:

> The worse his life was, or the harder the time he was having with his writing, the more he liked to be made to laugh. And he particularly loved facetiousness! One of his favourite times was during the Falklands War, since the capital of the Falklands is called "Stanley" and every day the papers had some wonderful headline like "First Man Into Stanley" or "Stanley Under Siege" or "Argentines Fly Flag at Stanley." He loved that, would never tire of it.[15]

He adored movie chit-chat and show-business stories, pumping film-score composer Elmer Bernstein for news from Hollywood, and musician Cynthia Millar for tales of New York, where she had played in the Broadway musical *Merlin*. "At one point he was so crazy about 'The Archers' [serialized radio show]," Cynthia says, "that if we were on the phone talking to each other, he'd say, 'Sorry, I have to go now: The Archers.' And 'Dynasty' [on television] was a big craze with him." He read dime-novels by the dozen, and gave Cynthia one he especially liked, about two sisters who swap lives.

"He was incredibly alive – the brain was always teeming, he was always up to something mentally, he always had something going through his head," a friend says, by way of explaining how Stanley thrived on gossip. "He wasn't ever unkind or dangerously indiscreet. He didn't spread news that everyone wouldn't have heard by five o'clock. He just knew it at nine o'clock, and he put it out," says Gill Coleridge, whose first telephone call at work many mornings was from Stanley, "eager to recount something he'd done the night before, tell some anecdote, always full of people and excitement, and often hinting about what X was doing or who Y was seeing now." "We called him 'The Gazette,' " says Henrietta. "If we wanted to fling the news about, he was always in the centre and he knew everything."

Nevertheless, people confided in him, sought his advice and trusted him to be discreet when discretion really mattered. He didn't let them down. "Either he could speak to no one else," Stanley wrote in his diary, about a new friend who vouchsafed a secret with far-reaching consequences, "or he trusted me a great deal. But I never told anyone what he said, and when the news was made public I acted as shocked as everyone else."

*

While Stanley loved knowing about others' private lives, he was highly selective in what he revealed about his own. His friends had to accept the fact that there was a great deal about Stanley that they did not know ("We took him for what he was, and rather marvelled," said Robert Kee[16]); and that there were a great many people who knew bits about him but didn't know all, and didn't know each other – the Duke of Devonshire and Kerstin Williams, for example: "I was fascinated by how he compartmentalized his life," says the Duke.

> I thought I knew him rather well, but after he was ill I used to go [to Charing Cross Hospital] and see him, and there were nearly always people there I never saw before. And how he found time for them all! It was certainly clear they loved him. He was an enormously loved man.[17]

Kerstin expresses a similar puzzlement:

> He had all his friends in pockets. I spent time with him almost every day, and I saw him with certain people but I didn't see him with other people whom I knew that he knew. He divided us all into various groups ... I never knew the reasons.[18]

The protective carapace, the mollusc shell he wrote about in his handbook on manners, served Stanley well; he retained a remarkable amount of privacy and control. Even his handwriting lent him cover, made it harder for him to be "prised open." It looked "as though a small and sober ant had tumbled into a bottle of blue ink and crossed and recrossed the page"[19] – perfectly legible but only through a magnifying glass. (Interestingly, it had been "normal" before, and assumed this notoriously minuscule size only after he had spent about three years in London expanding every other aspect of his life and personality.) A tactful copy-editor called it "decorative" but difficult, a perceptive friend called it "concealing – so tidy, but not the sort belonging to someone who wants you to know anything about him."[20]

Indeed, there were several aspects of his life that he did not want his friends to know about or dwell upon: his American past and family background, of course ("Boring!" was his usual response to inquiries, even from close friends, who desisted when further probing threatened to put him out of countenance); his financial situation; his Americanness itself. Selina Hastings says:

> He was so much accepted as an Englishman that someone at the dinner table might easily let slip an anti-American remark. And Stanley was only perturbed if the person then realized and apologized. He didn't like it to be remembered that he was American, and would much rather it had just passed. He was so nice about it.

Stanley's secretiveness about being a Jew was an understandable if regrettable aspect of his cultivation of an English character. From his wide reading, especially of Edwardian memoirs, he knew very well the forms of anti-Semitism among the "stylish" English, as well as among the English intelligentsia. (Virginia Woolf, after all, had turned to her husband when a point arose during a conversation at a Bloomsbury party, and said, "Let the Jew answer that." "I will if you ask me nicely," Leonard Woolf replied.)[21] And he had no reason to assume that they had changed much over the decades. Why risk being perceived as any more "different" than he already seemed? He had expatriated himself from one country; why risk even the slightest ostracism in another? Why risk genteel scorn or subtle stigmatizing, when his Jewishness need never come up? He would avoid the subject altogether, say nothing about it to anyone, not even to fellow Jews. In England this was easy enough to do: "Very few people in the circle he moved in were Jewish, and Jewishness is certainly not a subject they think about much. Jews in London, unlike in New York or Montreal, don't publicize it even to one another very often."[22]

An interesting contretemps occurred after Stanley's friend Susannah Phillips married a Canadian Jew, Chaim Tannenbaum. Chaim, who made no secret about being Jewish, made casual inquiries into Stanley's background. Was he really Scandinavian as his surname implied? Stanley wouldn't give. "Lots of laughter, rolling of eyes, pretend-indignant looks when Chaim pursued this line of questioning in a more roundabout way. Soon Chaim exclaimed: 'Stanley, you're Jewish!' Stanley was horrified and amused."[23]

"I never think of myself as [a Jew]," said Edwin Samuel Montagu, an Edwardian Englishman of considerable wealth and influence. "If people never thought of us as Jews, Jews like myself would forget all about it."[24] Stanley came as close to forgetting as possible, closer than Montagu and his peers were permitted to do in their day. Selina Hastings explains:

> In the Edwardian society everyone in the upper classes was very conscious of the Sassoons, the Rothschilds, the Oppenheimers, and the fact that they were new in society, the fact that they were usually very rich, the fact that they were all friends of the King – they were Jews, they were known to be Jews, they were known to be different. All right, they were accepted, but everyone knew very very well that there was a great gaping chasm between them and us. And with Stanley, he wasn't playing that part; he wasn't being Philip Sassoon. He was one of us. And by that I don't mean Christian. I mean he melded in so that he could have been like any of us – anything. And I think he knew that nobody gave a damn about it really.[25]

Perhaps. Yet his behavior and reaction to Chaim's questioning indicate otherwise. They suggest his sensitivity to the anti-Semitism in his milieu – an impersonal, "polite" anti-Semitism but as much a part of upper-class English life now as ever. He wanted so much to fit in, to be "one of us," that in effect he denied his heritage, his ethnicity, the historical-cultural ramifications of Jewishness. (The religious aspects he had dispensed with long ago; he wrote "Absolutely none" in the "Religion" box of a *Who's Who*-type questionnaire.) And with this denial he closed off an area of potential intimacy with Elmer Bernstein, Joyce Engelson and other Jewish friends who, had they known of their shared backgrounds, would have felt even closer to him.

It may be difficult (especially if one is a Jew and viscerally aware of how many of one's people involuntarily disappeared) to excuse Stanley's willed attempt to pass as a gentile, yet one must acknowledge the brilliance of his strategy given his overall aim: to achieve a perfect fit in English society, where to be a Jew is to be somehow un-English. An American acquaintance illustrates the point with an anecdote set at about the time Stanley arrived in London and began to forge his English character:

> I was having dinner with a certain noble lord twenty years ago, a real old Tory Lord Salisbury type, who said: "We really don't have a Jewish problem in England. Jews in England are thoroughly accepted. That embarrassing business back in the time of Edward, the expulsion of the Jews" – and he of course meant *not* Edward VII – "they're thoroughly accepted now. They're not really Jewish here in England, the Jews." And then there was a long pause and he looked up and said: "Of course they're not really English either."

"It is very disagreeable to know how Americans made their money. Now you have the world before you. You have only to enjoy," a European says to the eponymous hero of James's novel *The American*. Stanley's sentiments exactly. He was self-conscious about his financial situation, which looked sweet to others but had about as much substance as a chocolate meringue. He preferred not to discuss it with friends in London; there was quite enough of that discussion with family in Florida.

Although he claimed to Arlene (as justification for accepting "Family Welfare") that worry about money was a drain on creative energy, he nevertheless spent an extraordinary amount of time and energy wheedling it from parents, demanding it from publishers, and calculating just how little of it he could pay on his innumerable charge accounts to keep creditors off his back. ("Things are so bad I have had to pay my bills! Even Fortnum's rang me up. Mercifully I am beyond getting embarrassed. I waffled, hedged and then lied – as usual," he told Arlene.) He went from one credit crisis to the next, from one bailout and showdown with his father to another. A new budget was drawn up only to be overspent in a matter of weeks. The whole exercise became a lifelong game of the utmost complexity, a sort of high-wire act: capital acquisition through psychological manipulation; debt management as virtuoso feat.

The American financial agent who, for a time, managed Stanley's trust fund *in loco parentis* and doled out the interest payments, received this plea to dip into the principal after one of Stanley's book-research trips in New York and New England:

> I came back to London only to find the most staggering number of bills *plus* the impending obligations of the staggering expenses of staying in America, so in order to re-launch the budget balloon I must make a clean slate of both these branches of debt. Please do not hang your head and sigh! Can $—— be found in my account? Somewhere? This injection would make a clear path for the future, for the $—— per month regime which I fully intend to adhere to, for everyone's peace of mind.
>
> It is all well and good to point out that it is my money anyway, but the slight barrier of having to ask obliges me to reflect on this policy of taking and not replacing, which is scarcely fiscal planning. Any declaration of resolutions

satisfies no one, and I will not burden you with it. I will ring you next week to hear your ideas/orders/lamentations etc., on perhaps the faulty notion that forewarned is forearmed. What is slightly alarming is my complete ignorance of the vast expense of things to-day. I am dangerously out-of-touch, just in case you had not noticed. Damn! is my prime reaction.

His friends didn't know about his money problems, didn't know that he was almost always broke and lived on credit, that he had charge accounts everywhere not just for convenience but out of necessity. When he complained of being hard up from time to time (particularly to fellow writers), they thought he was only being companionable, trying to seem no better off than they were; certainly he spent money in a way they didn't and couldn't. (Was it credible that a man who had Harrods deliver dog bones, or invited you to dine at Claridge's at the drop of a hat, was financially strapped?) As Stanley's style of entertaining became grander and grander over the years, some people felt unable to reciprocate his hospitality properly and let their friendship lapse; most, however, delighted in the flamboyance and style of his extravagance, realized that he only wanted companionship in his self-indulgence, that he got pleasure from giving pleasure, and that the only quid pro quo was to accept his invitations and be good company. He had found the magic blend of altruism and hedonism, and it made him a splendidly generous friend, who gave with the easy naturalness of one who had all the money in the world and was grateful that you were there to share the good things it would buy.

If Stanley did not want people to talk about those aspects of his life he found boring (his American past), risky (his Jewishness), or unpleasant (his money problems), it was necessary to steer them toward topics that were acceptable

– and far more amusing. "He enlisted his friends in the con-
spiracy of Stanley Olson," says Susan Loppert, a longtime
co-conspirator in this involuntary exercise.* By talking about
his eccentricities and excesses, by celebrating them – as those
who knew him couldn't help doing – everyone reinforced the
image he had created of himself, and encouraged him in its
further elaboration.

His travel preparations, for example, took on legendary
proportions – especially if his destination was a great house
where a member of the staff would unpack his bags. First
came the wardrobe check to determine whether garment
alterations were required, either to accommodate changes
in style or his body shape. Then his luggage was sent to
Asprey's to be oiled and polished, after which someone from
the tailoring firm of Gieves & Hawkes arrived at the mews
to pack his suitcases. "Must go get my tissue paper ironed,"
he said in closing a hasty farewell note to Sybille Bedford
before he sailed aboard the QE2 to America.

He was only half-joking; he knew all this nineteenth-
century fuss was highly amusing to his friends, reason enough
to carry on with it ("Mr Olson wears a nightcap!" the Duke
learned to his delight, from the butler at Chatsworth, who
was "very, very fond of Stanley") were it not also genuinely
pleasing to Stanley himself.

From her office in the mews, Ann Dex had the closest
vantage point on the pre-departure activity. Just as Stanley
often interrupted her workday by parking his dog in her
office, he regularly commandeered her mother, Betsy Dex,
as his personal tailor:

Mum would come to the mews to type up my business

---

*Susan Loppert, South African-born art historian and critic, established Sotheby's
Cape Town office and was a prints specialist at Sotheby's, Bond Street. She met
Stanley in 1972, played tennis, listened to opera and gourmandized with him, and
was "dragooned into motoring him all over England, including an extraordinary
day with Stephen Tennant in Wiltshire."

correspondence twice a week, and he would nobble her at 6:30, offer her coffee and give her his things to be altered – trousers to be tapered, or let out when he put on weight, pyjama trousers to be hemmed because he had short legs. One time he got out all his evening clothes and the lapels were out of date and he told her to watch television for men wearing dinner jackets and tuxedos so she could copy the current lapel style. Mum was happy to do it, especially when she learned that he would wear her handiwork as a guest at Chatsworth.[26]

Mrs Dex expected and Stanley offered no fee for her services – "it was done from love" – though once he took her for tea at the Ritz, which she talked about for weeks. "He collected mothers," Ann says, "women who would fuss over him, 'do' for him – cook his favourite foods, take him on errands, walk his dog. And he had such charm that he always got away with it and was not resented."[27]

Everyone knew and chuckled about his "travelling sheets," which accompanied him on trains and ships and any place where he might experience a lesser degree of comfort than he was accustomed to at home. There his iron-and-brass Edwardian bed (single), painted silver and green, was made up with white sheets of pure linen – one of the twelve pair he bought "at knockdown prices" at Bloomingdale's. "The assistant had never sold a pair in the years she had worked there," he told an interviewer (shuddering at the thought of Americans' liking for colored, patterned sheets), "so of course I bought them all. I have the steward on the train make up my couchette with them. He has a fit!"[28]

Stanley's attitude toward his body and physical appearance was very complex – part childlike vanity, and part neurotic self-consciousness. Like a boy playing dressing-up games for the grown-ups, he loved being teased about his good looks, being told he had a "leonine" head, or that So-and-so had met him and said "What a good-looking man." Yet when he caught sight of himself on television, he wrote in his diary about what "an unattractive display of an example of humanity" he made. He did not like to be touched; would not remove his jacket in public, even during a heatwave; and to appear in a swimsuit – anywhere, ever – was out of the question.

Even on visits to hot, dusty southern Spain, Stanley appeared "in full-tie rig," says Frances Partridge. While visiting Tramores, the home of Jaime and Janetta Parladé in Andalusia, he and Sybille Bedford followed Frances on a long ramble through the countryside, which she knew well from previous visits. "Frances was the oldest of us and walked like a mountain goat," says Sybille. "It was tough. And Stanley had only city pumps with him." When eventually they had to ford a shallow river and he was forced to remove his shoes and socks and roll up his trousers, "the very whitest little legs came out," Frances says. "And rather pale-faced, he walked through." This was as undressed as friends ever saw him until his illness.

He shunned the camera usually, unless his dog was the ostensible focus of the picture, but posed occasionally for magazine photographers because he hoped the articles might promote his books. In 1986, worried that Macmillan would insist on having a photo for *Sargent* (he opposed on principle biographers' pictures appearing on book jackets), he wrote to Baron Fritz von der Schulenburg about a portrait shot taken two years before for *The World of Interiors*: "The one you did strikes me as about as good as one can get in that weird alchemy of turning a sow's ear into a silkish purse. And as I do not much care for trial by Kodak, you managed the minimum of pain."

Oddly enough, dandyism may have helped him reconcile his contradictory feelings about his physical presence. It allowed him to use his body even as he loathed it, to play up his excesses, corporeal and sartorial, and to justify them by the amusement they offered to others:

> Quite frankly I am rather bored doing serious combat with my clothes each morning. Always the drill, breathe in, more, more, then fasten trousers and watch the spillage: like leaping into a bath overfull and watching the water splash onto the carpet. I am bored – and it is the boredom of brute repetition – detesting sitting down and feeling my waistband rebel and rebel seriously. Hence my [tricycle]. Of course it is a joke. Of course it is idiotic, but above all it is very, very funny. People laugh when they see this huge mass struggling to balance all of itself on that pathetically midget seat. And then to see it in full tilt, with a spaniel holding on for dear life – or rather, just holding on. All told, I am v. well aware of its intense comic elements. And they are legion.[29]

As with his entire personality, Stanley's wardrobe, while distinctive, did not overstep the boundaries of "correctness"; rather, it stretched them. He strove to be original without being vulgar, identifiable without being conspicuous. He succeeded gloriously. From hat to house slippers, his made-to-order garments were superbly crafted from the finest materials; and apart from the occasional shirt with broad stripes of maroon and gold (remembered by Frances Partridge as lending "spice" to his wardrobe) or the "co-respondent" shoes he sported in his last years, they were impeccably, conventionally tasteful. Yet tucked inside were those red silk and red leather linings! – the Stanley touch, discreetly astonishing. And though he claimed that his preference for bow-ties was a practical measure – "they don't get in the way of fugitive cream sauce" – they too served to set him apart, since so few men wear them.

It was only because he knew so well the rules of dress that he could vary them, extend them, as he did. In his proposal for *The Gentleman's Handbook* – his "common-sense guide to the art of behaving (and appearing) like a gentleman, from haberdashery to honour, from soup spoons to sportsmanship, from etiquette to arrogance" – he spelled out the most crucial rule:

> Your attire ought to aim at and achieve one effect – lack of memorability, the precise opposite of the lady's mission. The key to this is colour. Nothing else matters; you can forget about fashion. You need not worry about being up-to-date, but you must take immense pains to be the correct hue. Town means dark colours – grey, navy blue or black (day and night). Country means lighter shades, the full range of pastoral values, at least during the day. Weekends in town equal the country, probably for no better reason than that you really ought to be in the country, while weekend dinners in the country equal town. It is a deceptively simple arrangement, designed to tame wild flamboyance and to suppress aggressive vanity.

Not surprisingly, Stanley's "common sense" guide, though indisputably witty and fun, was not what publishers Shuckburgh Reynolds had in mind for a contemporary courtesy manual. His sample chapters suggested to David Reynolds "that [Olson's] modern gentleman lives in the Wodehousian world of the 1930s, that his friends are called Sebastian and Humphrey, that he only attends butlered dinner parties where intelligent conversation is prohibited, [and] that at weekends he breakfasts only with other, similarly jacketed and trousered gentlemen."

When in 1983 Stanley planned to join his parents, brother, sister-in-law and nephews on a cruise in the wine country of France, he found himself at a loss: "I failed to ask you what I should wear on the yacht/barge," he wrote to his father:

> What do you suppose I can get away with on the waves? I mean, in what manner can I torture blue, grey and black into something like boating get-up? I've no casual clothes whatsoever. No soft-soled shoes. No knit shirts. And it is mad to buy them for five days. So, can I simply dress as if I were on land?

His wardrobe lacked other standard items as well. During the recovery period after his stroke, the hospital physiotherapist asked Stanley's Spanish housekeeper, Mrs Gonzalez, to bring a jogging suit and sport shoes from Stanley's flat. Mrs G. replied, with some hauteur, "*My* Mr Olson doesn't own such items!" Among other incongruities, they weren't in his price range: his shoes from New & Lingwood might cost fifteen hundred dollars a pair, his suits a couple of thousand.

Though he treasured his cufflinks collection – indeed, the settings and semiprecious stones would delight the eye of the most discerning jeweller – Stanley most prized his handkerchief collection, which he inventoried in a notebook by date of acquisition and current location (pocket/laundry/drawer):

> I spent two hours this evening tidying up my handkerchief drawers – it is the perfectly mindless sort of enterprise that makes one feel exceedingly virtuous. My handkerchiefs are desperately important to me – all 14 doz. – no, there are more than that, many more; I'd say about 20 doz, all catalogued and perfectly folded (recently). Just why they are important is hard to explain. I love fine things. I love luxury. I love slightly archaic things, and a handkerchief – not just any one either: voile, linen, etc. – is all of these. No journey is complete without buying a handkerchief or two. I suppose the collection began when the laundry lost my most precious pale blue Swiss voile one. I loved it and I miss it to this day. By strict accountancy the laundry will never lose another one: If they do, I charge them 3 times the purchasing price. They recently had to pay £15 for one handkerchief; they won't lose another quickly.[30]

In the course of refining his English personality, Gill Coleridge observes, "Stanley became a young old man. When he was thirty-five he was a sixty-five-year-old in his mannerisms – terribly funny and entertaining." Mirabel Cecil wrote about his enthusiasm for "the arcane, not to mention archaic, minutiae of English life":

> He has 12 different sizes of writing-paper, and three sizes of calling cards – the largest used for postal communication, "so I can write whole letters on them when I pay a bill" (his cheque book, by the by, is the size of a King Penguin paperback, so that he does not carry it around with him, not that that deters him from shopping). . . . There are his book plates, too. "I wanted them the size of a postage stamp, but they couldn't do them that small." So they are the size of *almost* two stamps, with the name engraved *just* off-centre: "I don't like things to be too centred – it's too anal."[31]

The same kind of calculated eccentricity and perverse individualism – along with a deep-seated love of the music – led to Stanley's ceaseless championing of Wagner. He liked him in part because so few of his friends did. "I still can't get the point of Mozart, I must tell you," he wrote to Arlene:

> Mozart crowds are much more boisterous than Wagner crowds and clearly a cut below. Mozart seems to flush out those who think they SHOULD go to the opera. . . . Everyone, thanks to my nursing or half-nelson, it depends which way you look at it, is now converting to Wagner. Mr. [Richard] Shone* . . . rang me up to boast how much he likes *Siegfried*, after years of downing the Master. Now two more arch-Antis have jumped on. Really if [Wagner] continues to get this popular I will learn to hate him.

Though the "archaic minutiae" of English life appealed to Stanley, the monumental bad taste of much contemporary London architecture provoked frequent "spleen-letting

---

*Richard Shone, associate editor of *The Burlington Magazine*, author of *Bloomsbury Portraits* (1976) and *Walter Sickert* (1988); closely involved in the saving of Charleston, and trustee of the Charleston Trust.

attacks," as he called them. "Bombs everywhere," he wrote during a wave of terrorist activity in 1975, "and they are not efficient enough to destroy really ugly buildings like the vile Hilton, that blot on Park Lane."[32] And after Robert Kee gave him a tour of the new BBC television headquarters in 1983, he wrote in his diary:

> The building looks like a train depot from America in the 1930s. It is painfully dreary – grey, and very fashionably *art moderne* in style, determined to look foul in a few months . . . a classic example of architects getting beyond themselves and forgetting people altogether. The canal side is fine, with boiled-egg motif.

It is unlikely that Stanley was any less opinionated about politics and politicians than about music or architecture; his sense of the absurd was far too keen. But since his friends' politics were as varied as his friends themselves, he took care not to offend – especially because, as an American, his outspoken criticism and comments about British public affairs and personalities might seem impertinent. Frances Partridge voiced surprise at "his really rather left-wing politics, which I liked because mine are"; others among his friends might well have assumed he sympathized with their more Conservative views. Diary entries make clear his loathing for Mrs Thatcher, in any case, and a 1984 visit from her American counterpart (whose rubber likeness amused his dog) elicited this sardonic entry:

> Saw President Reagan en convoy in Seymour Street – 12 cars, swarming police, pressmen in a coach, Secret Service men draped over an open limousine, helicopter above, and in the centre the chief clown. Circuses were never like that when I was young.

Ironic detachment was the wisest stance for him to take on political affairs, and usually he got away with it. He was ill-equipped to handle political dogmatism face-to-face; it made him defensive, sparked tirades in which he made claims as sweeping (if not as humorless) as those of his interlocutor:

A friend is now in London vintage my undergraduate days – a specialist on Chinese foreign policy. You might picture the scene: me wallowing about in a vat of total ignorance and disinterest [sic], beating my gums about something that could not be more dull. And I am getting rather tired that I should be made to feel guilty for not caring about something. Not China, but matters of one's fortune occluding the misfortune of others. Fancy being told "Biography is a capitalist art form!" Well, at least I got the "art form"; that's more than most. Or maybe a "capitalist indulgence." How distressing. I absolute- ly refuse to pay attention to politics or history – both ignore people. And people are the most important thing. I refuse to vote. I refuse to look at the newspapers. I refuse to listen to the news – whatever that is.[33]

Notwithstanding its distinct rewards, social life – being a host, being a guest – is arduous, time-consuming (and expensive) work, especially if one has perfectionist standards, as Stanley did. But it was just the sort of work he was cut out to do. "He was the soul of hospitality, generosity, and knowing how to give pleasure and to receive pleasure," says Sybille Bedford, extolling Stanley's talent as host of intimate dinners in Montagu Mews as well as his help at her garden parties for thirty in Chelsea. "He would be my barman. He would do the drinks, he would open the door, he would handle the ice – all with extreme competence."

In the mews he liked to have no more than four at dinner, where a typical feast – if not quite so Lucullan as the menu he prepared for Sue Baring – might be quail eggs, celeriac, Parma ham, *bollito misto*, and chocolate gateau. Or, on a more formal occasion, lobster consommé, duck Baron, and *bombe chocolat* with kirsch and pralines. And of course a bounteous flow of champagne and good wines. Even when guests returned home at the end of an evening, they might find themselves, as did Richard and Leonée Ormond, "in a delightful afterglow – with those ravishing violets and the delicious cheese" he had sent along with them.

His triumphs as host were the culmination of days if not weeks of meticulous planning, and unusual insight into what his guests would enjoy. (Perhaps because he so loved comfort and pleasure himself, such acuteness came naturally to him.) Yet no matter how elegant the menu and presentation, the mood was always warm and informal; one might be asked to give a stir to the risotto while he fed the dog, or to make the coffee because he claimed ignorance of the mysteries of brewing. There was no stuffiness, no servants; in fact, he was embarrassed enough to write in his diary on the occasion when his housekeeper (whose feelings he didn't want to hurt by insisting that she leave) imposed a ridiculous formality upon him and his lunch guest:

[When Heywood Hill arrived], as luck would have it, Mrs. G. was here and there is nothing she likes more than serving at table, which in my flat is rather mad, and worse, pretentious and genteel. ... I think he might have been offended. ... Of course I hate that extra-genteel approach to life. It makes me cringe. But luxury – that is a different story.

As for luxurious entertaining, Stanley's standards were developed and refined through observation of some of Britain's greatest hosts. In Nancy Mitford's *The Pursuit of Love* a suave Frenchman tells a young Englishwoman in Paris:

... society people ... have made a fine art of personal relationships and of all that pertains to them – manners, clothes, beautiful houses, good food, everything that makes life agreeable. It would be silly not to take advantage of that.

... You should never despise social life – that of high society –
I mean, it can be a very satisfying one, entirely artificial of course,
but absorbing.[34]

Although Stanley the Outsider had a realistic notion
of his place in the English social hierarchy, he relished the
time he spent exploring the upper boundaries, going where
others in his position were not likely to go, gaining access
through the power of his personality, his wit, charm and
enthusiasm. And he took full advantage of the opportunities
offered by high society when they came his way, focusing
his scholar's eye on every "agreeable" aspect of life there
(down to requesting from the housekeeper Mrs Carr a
conducted tour of the Chatsworth House linen cupboards)
but taking a special interest, an almost obsessive interest, in
observing his hosts' behavior toward guests, their efforts to
make guests comfortable, to give guests pleasure. He seemed
almost surprised at the attention they devoted to this aspect
of entertaining, and remarked upon it frequently in his
diary:

Went to a dinner party at Diana Phipps's in Connaught
Square. The guests: Lord and Lady X; Countess E, some
Italian (?) aristo intellectual who was completely delightful;
some Dr. from Birkbeck who was just intellectual and v.
charmless with it; me (no comment, though I ought to
add that our poor hostess must have been dredging an old
address book to get me); and Carl and Estelle Reiner, the
film producer and his soon-to-be singer wife (and my word
they were the stars).

Carl Reiner made a great success by 1) calling Lady
X "Your Highness" (jokingly) then failing to, which Lord
X noticed; 2) by ad libbing Shakespeare perfectly; 3) by
possessing brute sound wit – common sense. One would
have to be made of stone not to fall for his humour (though
I never did like the Dick Van Dyke Show, despite its seminal
position in the history of TV – and is *that* a compliment?) C.

Reiner made himself very agreeable by turning to the maid and complimenting her – She beamed! And what a pretty face she had. Clive James came in and browbeat us with his standard gymnasium-equipment phrases, all very tidy and all very heavy. He is clever, I must confess.

But our hostess impressed me a lot. I was flattered to be asked, for a start, and I was struck by her style – *style not for its own sake but for the comfort of people* [emphasis added].

Friends often teased Stanley about his friendship with peers of the realm and his visits to stately homes. When asked what he talked about with such a celebrity-aristocrat as the Duke of Devonshire, he replied simply: "We both are trying to grow white roses." But their conversations extended beyond horticulture to historical scandals of the Edwardian period (the Tranby Croft baccarat affair), contemporary novels (Stanley interested the Duke in reading Rebecca West's *This Real Night*), art (the Duke asked Stanley to be his "mentor" at the Prado Museum in Madrid), and libraries (the Duke's library is famous).

"Stanley was interested in everything and everyone," the Duke says, surely realizing that a particular focus of Stanley's wide-ranging curiosity was the whole system of entail and primogeniture by which he, Andrew Cavendish, had become, after his brother's death in the war, the Eleventh Duke of Devonshire and the inheritor of a vast amount of spectacular real estate in Europe, including Lismore Castle in Ireland, where Stanley's visit occasioned this diary entry:

The burden of Lismore is the burden of genealogy: the Cavendishes have not had any spare sons for a long time. After all they got this house 200 years ago because of that scarcity. Andrew has inherited it as the 2nd son, from his uncle, but then AD's brother died so he got Chatsworth, Compton Place, Bolton as well. Now AD has only one son. So it begins all over again. Such a predicament must be the greatest indictment against this male-orientated and unrealistic system.

Chatsworth, the Duke and Duchess of Devonshire's magnificent house in Derbyshire – a 175-room palace, really, parts of which are open to the public who visit by the tens of thousands – boasts among its art collection a famous Sargent painting ("The Acheson Sisters") that Sargent's biographer simply had to see. When he did, for the first time, one memorable day in May 1981, he went not as a paying visitor but as the invited weekend guest of the Devonshires. It was a turning point in his life, and everyone he knew heard about it, especially his parents:

> I have just come back from staying at Chatsworth, probably the grandest house in the world. The whole weekend was of such a superior nature that I could never hope to explain it adequately, especially not here. One of my fellow guests was Harold Macmillan which only goes to show how Sargent is helping me to get so above myself. I travelled back to London with Macmillan, and every toady on the platform fell over themselves to get near him. The porter went to get my luggage, looked at my luggage tag and spotted at once that I was a nobody, and did not pick up the bag! Speaking about being put into one's place! There were 20 staying in the house; each had a private bath and the household was not strained in the least. It was not at all real life. We ate off gold plate on Saturday night and the BBC filmed the entire weekend. The house was open to the public throughout the stay and my embarrassment at crossing through doors marked 'PRIVATE' was extreme. Still, not surprisingly, I would not have missed it for the world. *The one extraordinary aspect about it was how much attention was given to giving pleasure to everyone* [emphasis added]. There was no instance when the notion of Them and Us ever arose: every improvement to the house was made to improve the sensation given to the paying visitor. It was a great eye-opener.

These country house weekends are very hard work. One has

to make conversation every meal: first to the person on one's right, then with the next course, to the person on one's left and then vice versa. At the end of 10 or so meals one's talent for talk has fairly collapsed but at no moment can one give way. And it isn't as if the public side of these weekends is the only area where standards cannot drop. What with butlers laying out clothes [down to the hanky folded into the pajama jacket pocket] and drawing baths, one's behaviour has to remain as uniformly near-perfect as possible all the time. On Monday I went straight back to bed.

Stanley's warm friendship with the Duchess (*née* "Debo" Mitford) included enlisting her aid in his Sargent research. A London friend of his, on hearing of this, wrote:

Few biographers can boast a duchess for a researcher. It reminds me of some lines from "Rape of the Lock" (the first canto, I think): 'What rare author couldst induce / A well-bred duchess to research a book; / What rarer still (durst he boast?) / A Mitford sis to have a look?' It doesn't scan, I grant you that, and the meaning is not quite clear, but then Pope never was particularly consistent (too much social life!).[35]

Though in letters to his American family and friends he couldn't help boasting a bit – who wouldn't? – about the grand company he sometimes kept, Stanley had no illusions about where he fit in the scheme of things, as this diary entry about another country weekend among the high-born makes clear:

. . . That night at dinner which dissolved mercifully into bridge (mercifully because I'm excluded) there was some attempt at conversation and Dame X showed in her views all the originality of a Mars bar. Apart from being violently pro-Mrs. T which of course she has a right to be, she has a form of conservatism that shows up the right-wing mentality as being slack. She has no knowledge of books, music, art, and puts out not the slightest twinge that something might be lacking. But it must be owned I show the same ignorance for her strong suits – racing, fishing, sport and genealogy. I am the odd fish here and make no mistake. I've been given a glimpse into the strangest territory known to the human condition. It is agreeable tourism, but shows one at once how very much work a snob must have to do [in order] to be part/make himself part. This is a world into which admission comes by birth, not achievement or effort. Nothing can overcome that requirement and snobs must turn themselves into court jesters – forever on parade.

He may have felt the "odd fish" in "strange territory" at times, but he was a most agreeable tourist while there. He surprised the Duke of Devonshire on a visit to Ireland by agreeing to go fishing. "I can see it even now," the Duke says, "Stanley looking rather mournful on the river bank." And did he catch anything? "A stone."

Stanley's own diary puts it like this:

[Feb. 9–12, 1985 – Lismore, County Waterford] Went fishing – has a nice archaic ring to it. Caught a lot of the bottom of the river to be honest; my hands were blue my lungs were frozen and I loved every single minute of it.

PART III

THE MAN OF LETTERS

He might give the appearance of a dilettante with his large round figure, silk-lined jackets, love of good food and wine and discursive anecdotes; but when it came to writing all was honed to the essentials. His mannered style was not the result of self-indulgence but of acute powers of perception.

Richard Ormond[1]

What of himself an author puts into a book can never be surely judged, even if he himself confirms it, for he does not know what unconsciously he has done.

William Sansom[2]

The most delicate and humane of all the branches of the art of writing has been relegated to the journeymen of letters; we do not reflect that it is perhaps as difficult to write a good life as to live one.

Lytton Strachey[3]

I t is no small wonder that Stanley, so dedicated to friends and social life, also managed to produce in a seventeen-year period one book-length dissertation on Bloomsbury, two thoroughly researched and well-crafted biographies, an edited volume of historically significant documents, and a miscellany of reviews and articles. But he was determined to write as well as he lived – even when that involved shelving his "very comfortable and spoiled life" for bouts of work.

He never shelved it for long. Stanley wrote – like he ate and drank and attended opera – in binges. Balance rarely obtained; excess was the rule. A self-confessed lazybones, he designed strict work regimens (usually involving pre-dawn labor, so he wouldn't miss too much of the worldly day of shops and telephone calls and lunches out) and made valiant if short-lived attempts to hold to them – once even asking dinner guest Robert Kee to set his watch-alarm for 11:15. "The alarm went off and we all left Stanley's flat," recalls Selina Hastings. "He was *terribly* disciplined about that sort of thing." For the moment – and to set a good example for a new biographer like Selina. The following evening he might carouse till the wee hours with a group of friends who were completely unknown to his literary guests of the night before.

"Gone are the days of dinner every night of the week.

Meeting people for drinks, tea, lunch – all are strictly pro-scribed," he wrote to an overseas friend, just after beginning work on his Sargent biography. But in the next paragraph: "I will be in Bayreuth for The Ring this summer. And there is the performance of Lohengrin next week . . . well, I certainly am a hypocrite when I say my old life is over. Never mind." And as postscript: "How does one have time for friends *and* work? One always suffers."[4] Though a lament endemic to those who must create in seclusion, in Stanley's voice it conveyed unusual poignancy. "He *lived* for people," says Gill Coleridge, and he suffered when the weight of guilt and deadlines condemned him to forced labor and solitary confinement. Living well came naturally; writing well was so difficult that making a career of it seemed a form of masochism:

> I am certain that writing anything is like having the builders in: comprehensive torture hotly followed by disbelief that one ever voluntarily endured such pain. It seems nothing less than a miracle if the paint stays up on the wall. I remember actually thinking that all the words would fall off the paper once I lifted up the typescript. Self-inflicted lunacy, if you ask me.[5]

He was a perfectionist about writing, as about everything worthwhile in his life. "Is it not one of the finest injustices that flawless, smooth, graceful prose – the sort that reads like a nib on rollerskates – is the very prose one dies over?" he asked Sybille Bedford.[6] Each time he sat down to write, it was such prose he aimed for.

Stanley was frequently compared to Henry James, and not only because they were expatriate Americans who found their niche as men of letters in England. John Grigg, reviewing *Sargent* for *The Listener* said: "Mr Olson . . . writes in a dis-tinctly Jamesian style, though not always with the master's ability to be, against all the odds, comprehensible."[7] And

Meryle Secrest, in the *Philadelphia Inquirer* wrote: "Given such an accomplished portrait, it seems churlish to quibble, and yet one wishes the narrative did not seem so transparently modeled after a novel by Henry James."[8]

Stanley was aware of the dangers he courted: "My favourite author is Henry James who is not the best possible model for a young writer, but he is, I believe, the most stylish."[9] And he knew that Sargent himself had fallen victim to a similar adulation in his youth: ". . . throughout the 1880s the loud, reverberating echoes in John's paintings led directly back to Velazquez. . . . the very strength of these performances invited critics to announce his sources."[10] But Stanley so admired what has been called James's "controlled excessiveness" – and it dovetailed so well with his own temperament – that he couldn't resist attempting it from time to time, as here where he describes the differing social propensities of two of Sargent's friends. The Smyth sisters, he says, were

> a sort of beef-cattle who lowered their eyes on the surrounding fences, taking quite different measurements. Mary was calculating how many could graze in her pasture and Ethel was kicking to get out, and their success, measured in contrary fat-stock analysis, was considerable.[11]

Nor could he resist archaic Jamesian spellings: "week-end," "to-day," "pic-nic." A nineteenth-century reader looking at one of Stanley's unedited drafts would have felt quite at home.

He worshipped the Master and everybody knew it. Cynthia Millar (introduced to Stanley when she came to work at Heywood Hill's bookshop, where he obtained his twenty-four-volume New York Edition of James's work) thinks Stanley would not have paid her special attention had she not told him her address:

> We first became friends because I was living with my grand-

mother in the big mansion-flat block in Kensington where Henry James had lived. Granny's apartment was directly above his, and since all the rooms are the same shape, Stanley could come and figure out how it would have been for James, sitting in the window looking out from his writing desk. He was really thrilled.

If as literary stylist Stanley put people in mind of James, he also bore a resemblance to James as gentleman. Intensely sociable bachelors – witty, cosmopolitan, with refined nineteenth-century tastes – both men were "outsiders" in England, and keen observers of human behavior. The hundred years that separated their births were oddly telescoped by Stanley's penchant for James's cultural and historical period, and his scholarly recreation of it in his books and his daily life.

Of course Stanley reveled in the comparison, even subtly encouraged it; a few friends got the impression that he, like James, came of wealthy old New England stock and had gone to Harvard. Oddly, though, in *Sargent* Stanley sounds rather annoyed with James, as if he were describing a rich but pesky, busybody uncle always banging on about something. Perhaps this reflects his scholarly objectivity; perhaps a need to cut his heroes down to size.

"Quality is now a four-letter word," Stanley declared, bemoaning the deterioration in publishing standards while consoling a writer-friend for "evilly inept" editorial cuts made to her magazine article. "The days of [Harold] Ross and the great editors of journals are long gone, damn it. We *have* to put up with mediocrity."

But of course he didn't put up with it – at least not without first lodging a stunning complaint. Once he even went so far as to return a book to a major London publisher:

I would like a refund. It is, I think I can safely say, one

Front row, l. to r.: *Arlene, Stanley.* Back row, l. to r.: *Norman, Cousin Fred (c. 1950).*

Cousins' birthday party: Stanley seated at head of table; Phyllis in foreground, second from left (c. 1953).

Stanley, Arlene, Norman (c. 1952).

A dog-fearing Stanley and Andy the poodle sit as far apart as possible, with Arlene and Norman (c. 1956).

The Culver cadet joined by Arlene and Norman at his graduation dance (1965).

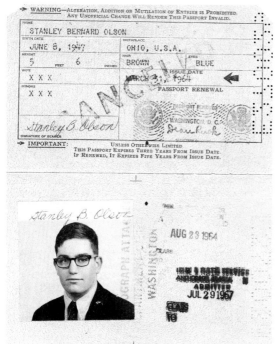

Passport to Europe and Asia.

The newly expatriated Stanley makes a visit to family in Akron (c. 1970).

Wuzzo in his dickey seat, with Stanley and the tricycle (c. 1974).

Stanley's handwriting in 1975, about midway in its shrinking process; by 1986 it was smaller by half.

Cooking with Philippa Pullar (1979).

Stanley's "silkish purse" portrait photo, commissioned from Fritz von der Schulenburg for use in publicizing Sargent *(1986).*

*Stanley at Rebecca West's grave,
Brookwood Cemetery, near
Woking in Surrey (1986).*

*Stanley and Sue Baring
in Venice,
(Christmas 1982).*

Family dinner during Stanley's last visit to America (January 1986).

Stanley on a "pic-nic" at Parliament Hill Fields just weeks before his 1986 stroke.

of the worst edited books I have ever come across; that is, however, if it were edited at all. . . . All these problems [which were spelled out in detail] are the fault of the publisher, thus I return the book to you. Had the author an editor who had read the book, there would not be the problems which have, clearly, so annoyed one reader at least. Thank you very much.

And if a friend's work were savaged in the press, Stanley took to his typewriter in high dudgeon indeed. "It was remarkably cheap of you to criticize Sybille Bedford's novels for what they were *not*," he wrote to a reviewer:

This line of literary criticism was favoured by the late I A Richards and was agreed by most intelligent people to be an idiotic form of logic.

Your reviews were a disgrace, not because there was a difference of opinion, but because you used [her] novels to advance your own social comments. This is reprehensible, and utterly unforgivable.

He excoriated another reviewer for being rude and ill-informed in describing author Delia Millar "merely as the wife of the Surveyor of the Queen's Paintings (from which one must, I suppose, infer a sort of qualification gained at the altar)," when the lady herself "is a very eminent scholar, which would have been evident had you read the book! Honestly, you of all people ought to have known better."

If literary journalism was in a sorry state, contemporary biography was "an utter shambles":

It is nothing more than a wonderful library performance, a dance on sources without any attempt at literature. Why do modern biographers think research alone equals a life? They have got tremendously arrogant, suffering from that Victorian notion that their efforts are reference works meant to stand the test of time – hang the simple detail the book is meant to be read, not consulted. Oh God! I despair.[12]

(He had a chance to preach on this subject to a larger audience when the prestigious American literary quarterly *Antaeus* published his essay "On Biography" which then won inclusion in an anthology of the year's best essays.[13])

On the other hand, no one could be more praiseful than Stanley of good writing, editing and publishing. He so admired Jean Strouse's 1980 *Alice James: The Life of the Brilliant but Neglected Younger Sister of William & Henry James* that he made a point of calling on Jonathan Galassi, then a young and unknown Houghton Mifflin editor, to congratulate him for publishing it. He heaped praise on Jean Strouse herself, in a fan letter and a review he wrote for *The Observer*, and bought a dozen copies of the book to press upon friends. In 1985 when she received a Guggenheim fellowship he noted in his diary: "Good news. She is the best biographer around."

To writer-friends in London he gave not only praise but direct assistance. He arranged a commission for musician Cynthia Millar to write a children's book about Bach, and then gave her his office – "the most restful, blissful place to work," she says – to write it in while he went to America. When Selina Hastings began her first biography, he shared everything he'd learned about filing and cross-referencing notes, and lectured her on the importance of good posture and a proper typing chair. They were close writing buddies, often the first readers of each other's work: "He rang me up nearly every day when we were both working on books, to see how I was getting on. If I said, 'Awful,' he would make me go and see him with the bit I was working on and read it to him." His suggestions were always helpful, she says.

> And I've never forgotten what he did when I finished my book [*Nancy Mitford*]. As soon as it was done, I left the manuscript with him to read and went up to North Wales, an eight-hour drive away. By the time I got there, Stanley had left seven or eight telephone messages saying, "It's wonderful,

it's wonderful," and "please have her call Stanley the minute she gets there."

Having been in her situation himself, he didn't want to cause her a single extra moment of anxiety through his delay. Nor would he permit her to be any less considerate of another writer: when he learned that she had refused a doctoral student's request for an interview about Nancy Mitford, pleading an imminent deadline and not a second to spare, he was "profoundly shocked":

He said, "That's an abominable way to behave, and *of course* you will see her. And you must never never turn down anybody. You mustn't withhold material unless it is essential to your book. You never know when you're going to need help from somebody else. We depend on other people's help just as they depend on ours."[14]

Even before he completed his Ph.D., early in 1973, Stanley knew that a free-lance writing career meant continued financial dependence on his family (though it wasn't clear that his family knew that, yet). Book reviews about Bloomsbury, and magazine articles about chocolate meringues might bring in sufficient income to support Wuzzo's high standard of living, if he were lucky, but no more than that. And a teaching job – or anything else Stanley qualified for – would no more support his desired life-style than writing; besides, he loathed what he called "Universityism." What was the point of taking a job he hated, if he would still have to ask his family for handouts?

"I reached an all-time low the other day," he wrote to his sister, "and applied for a job at Harrod's, at the grand wage of £16 a week. And it is a 45 hour week, so it works out to just under a dollar an hour. One book review pays more than that." To his parents he sent a characteristic plea for money: "I have been budgeting myself scrupulously, but London has become very very expensive; my earnings, which are erratic, do take the pressure off considerably. How wretched to moan about money when I am so much better off than everyone else I know." He couldn't bear the thought of leaving cherished friends, he said, or his flat; it was impossible to think of giving up all he had struggled to achieve in his new life.

They came through, once again, with a generous if reluctant bailout. But Stanley knew that unless he had a big break soon, his London gig was up. Just then a *deus ex machina* appeared in the form of Elinor Wylie, American poet. The rest is history, and best told by him:

THE PROGRESS OF ELINOR WYLIE[15]

My career as a biographer began with a missed airplane, and I was not the one who missed it. My London agent [Gill Coleridge's associate Giles Gordon] was trapped in New York one day longer than he intended, and was caught, by the man who eventually became my publisher, wandering around Fifth Avenue. They went for a drink. "Do you know anyone who might like to write the life of Elinor Wylie?" was the publisher's parting question. It was carried across the Atlantic and put to me.

My reaction, born out of unemployment, was tepid excitement. I knew I was not the first person to be asked the question [Anne Sexton, for one, had said no], but I resolved to be the last. Yes, I said, I would consider the idea. After all, no publishers seeking an employee or a writer were breaking down my door, fresh as I was from university. I went to the Reading Room of the British Museum, then to the London Library, reading everything I could lay my hands on about Elinor Wylie. She emerged from the few published scraps as a modern subject rivalled only by Katherine Mansfield: short life, tragic death, and great mystery. Onto these similarities Elinor piled wealth, very great beauty, a string of husbands and suicides, and quite remarkable, if currently unrecognized, skills as a writer. My excitement grew. We seemed suited for partnership. I was living in England. Elinor wanted to die in England, and I was only taking over where she left off. She brushed, very slightly, a period I was familiar with. But there remained the worry – what would a man make of this essentially feminine creature? Her vanity always displayed itself, with great success, to men. Perhaps a male biographer was not altogether unsuitable. I sent in my outline and it was accepted, at once.

Contract signed, desk cleared for the start, I went to Paris to meet Elinor's niece. She had been born six months before Elinor died. There would not be much in the way of reminiscences, I warned myself. What there had been was a welter of expectant potential biographers littered before me. My welcome in the Marais was a sigh: *another* future biographer. My contract alone stood me ahead of the competition. The niece had no papers at all, and fewer photographs. If I were expecting an Aspern paper cache my expectations were not satisfied. She could only help me with a sheet of paper, permitting me access to Elinor's papers in public collections, notably at Yale and at the Berg Collection at the New York Public Library. Any papers that had once been in family hands were now safely stored away in the hands of a young professor in a minor mid-western university who, some fifteen years before, had carried them off from Paris with the promise that he would date and transcribe them. He never got around to it. He never got around to returning them either. Urgent requests flew across the Atlantic. Silence. Legal advice was sought and action threatened. Silence. The papers remained invisible. I begged. I enlisted support. And I continued to hope. He had a Ph.D. student who was attempting to publish her thesis on Elinor. I despaired. These invisible papers loomed as the key to my work. They gained, in their absence, very great importance. Then word reached me, through a fourth party, that the papers would not be sent to me. All hope was dashed.

I placed advertisements in newspapers, trying to locate anyone still living who might have known Elinor. I got extraordinary replies. "No, I did not meet Elinor Wylie, but my mother once had a book of hers. I remember her reading it with some pleasure". "When Elinor died I wrote a poem about her," another eager assistant informed me. "If you want that poem I can let you see it". These offers of help spilled in. "I once saw Elinor Wylie at a party, but I don't remember much of her. I see you are living in London. Could you look up a relative of mine?" Another excitedly informed: "I know nothing at all about Elinor Wylie. But I am just about to publish a book of poems. Should I put your name down for a copy?" Then the most helpful response of all reached me. "I met Edith Wharton once on a train. I was a small child and I liked her. Perhaps this is of some help to you. Could you please send me some stamps?"

My despair reached new heights. No letters. No friends. I did not know what to do. I planned to go back to America for a few months to do the main body of research in university libraries, but there were still dreadful gaps in my material. Just as I was about to leave to catch the liner in Gibraltar (I have never suffered from an acute sense of geography), the telephone rang. It was Paris. "The papers from Ohio have just arrived. We are off to Mexico in a few days. Can you come over and make your notes? By the way, there does not seem to be much in them as far as we can see".

I could not possibly get to Paris in time to intercept Elinor's relatives without missing my liner. All my appointments in America were confirmed. I had found some friends of Elinor's – and they were far from young; they could not be let down. Time was against me on all accounts. I did not know what to do. After dozens of telephone calls, a friend of a friend said she would be willing to undertake the job of photocopying the papers. But it would be very expensive, and there might be nothing in the papers at all.

I sailed to America dreaming of these letters, hoping that they would unravel many mysteries. I had not been in New York in years, and pictured myself shivering in the freezing wastes of Manhattan. My fear of the cold, the mountains of snow, and the blustery gales made me take hundreds of sweaters, gloves, hats. As a result I lumbered myself with a great deal of luggage. When I docked, New York was a frozen wasteland and I sighed that my prediction had been correct. But the next day it turned to near-tropical heat. There was no way to turn off the radiator in my room. No breeze came through the window when I finally managed to open it. I was sweltering. My clothing was all of the thickest wool or flannel. And there I was with five vast cases and a huge radio which my father had sent to me. There was simply no way to carry it all on the next stages of my journey. I started sending suitcase after suitcase back to London, not with notes but with clothing. I tried to economise every gesture, even to the point of getting on the wrong train. There were no porters anywhere. No one offered the slightest help, except perhaps a laugh. It was maddeningly pathetic. Just loading all the luggage on and off trains was exhausting me.

And on top of it all I was not making much headway with my research. I found that I had a lot of partners. One woman rang me up saying that she was doing a "feminist" biography of Elinor. We *had* to meet. That meant one afternoon gone. Another woman found me and said, in a somewhat haughty manner, that she was doing a book about Elinor's ghost. And there was so much material in the libraries I consulted, I could not possibly read it all, even if I could photocopy everything. Somehow I managed to get no closer to my subject, but with alarming swiftness I got further away.

Before I started my research I determined that the best way to take notes was in bound notebooks. They would stay tidy. Nothing would get lost. But what I had not foreseen was that each notebook would contain material spread out through Elinor's life: I might copy the details of a birth certificate on the reverse side of a page containing a poem she wrote just before she died. Though these notebooks looked tidy, lined up like little soldiers and increasing in number every week, they concealed the considerable chaos inside. It got to the point that I simply could not find notes I knew I had taken. My organisation was appalling. I was wasting more time finding what I had than taking down new material. I even thought of rewriting every note I had taken. Then I decided that a card file would work as my index, kept in strict chronological order, to my numerous notebooks.

My time in America was running out. I had sent back far too many winter clothes. By the time I got to Yale I was shivering again. I only had time to chart what had to be done. And as I was coming to the end of my researches at Yale, one very helpful library assistant drew my attention to the files of *uncatalogued* papers. My heart sank. I was beginning to wish that my agent had caught his airplane after all. I prayed for some enormous fire, setting me free of all these papers. I cursed Elinor's husbands for keeping so much. I cursed Elinor. Why couldn't she have kept a diary, written an autobiography; why couldn't she be more cooperative? My sadness advanced to deep depression. What was I doing wasting my life writing *her* life? What was I doing leading the life of some prisoner of library hours and a captive of overheated rooms? Surely there was more to life than this.

I tried to shelter myself from the tedium of the job itself. I wrote with blunt pencils, then reverted to very sharp ones. I started taking notes on loose sheets of paper. Then I returned to my bound notebooks. Then I was determined to type everything. I was convinced I would never finish. I drank too much once the library closed. Then I decided to work harder, going to the library in the evening once the manuscript collection shut. I was *too* tired. My vision began to blur. I told myself I wouldn't need certain documents. I started making lists of what had to be done, ticking each off almost before it was finished. But my one sustained emotion was despair. There was no way to minimize the enormous job I had taken on. I refused to trust research assistants; in order to have some confidence, I had to see everything myself.

I got back to London, exhausted, and found the Paris papers waiting for me. I tore open the envelopes with great excitement and read the endless sheets of paper. My heart sank. Not one letter in Elinor's handwriting. Her sister and her brother's letters were there, but none by Elinor. Another dead-end. I wrote to Paris, begging them to find Elinor's letters. No reply. I telephoned. A strange voice answered. The apartment had been sold. No, they did not know where the previous tenants had gone. I became frantic. My one direct link to Elinor had vanished.

I drew up a letter to my publisher. I had wasted one full year. There was absolutely no hope of ever finishing the book. There was not enough material. The library collections, when placed together, traced Elinor's life from 1908 to 1910, then took up the story again at 1920 and continued to her death in 1928. Nothing for the childhood and nothing for the decade 1910–1920. It was obvious no biography was possible. I knew I would have to pay back my advance, and I did not have the money. I could do no more work. I had to give it up.

Then a letter arrived, postmarked "California". Elinor's niece had moved to America and had, finally, got the letters I wanted. Would I like to come to California, she asked, and take notes. This was out of the question. Far too expensive. My publisher somehow managed to get them photocopied and sent on to me. After eighteen months of work the most important documents for the biography were on my desk. Most of them, however, were undated. They were in no order. Elinor's handwriting, I had learned, was never easy to decode. But at least I had them. The crucial gaps were filled in. I could start writing.

I found writing a long procedure, but steady. I woke up every morning, appallingly early some would say, and traveled the very considerable distance from my bedroom to my sitting-room. There I sat in my dressing-gown, summer and winter, writing throughout the morning. The postman laughed when he saw me at the door. The neighbours refused to suppress their amusement over the fact that I was "working". In the afternoons I would go to the library to do more research. It was a wonderful routine – slow, but comforting.

The first three chapters were written at a breakneck pace: three months for each. Then the next three chapters spilled out only marginally more quickly, and by the time I reached the final decade of Elinor's life, things began to move slightly more swiftly. The moment I finished the complete first draft I turned around and started all over again.

I reread the first chapters with considerable horror. I had made the fatal mistake of waiting too long to begin writing. They were disastrously over-written. Embarrassingly bad. I shuddered. And I simply could not face making the whole journey all over again. I instantly decided that it was up to my editor to tell me what to do. I volunteered to come to America and go over the entire first draft with him. It was the summer of 1977 – the hottest on record. It was impossible to work. The thermometer refused to go any lower than 100 degrees. My hotel room had no air-conditioning and my editor had no time. I was sent packing with a few trenchant suggestions about improvements. So, for the next three months I sat reworking every sentence in the whole thing. Every day, for eight hours, Saturday and Sunday included, I combed the entire text. Towards the end I thought nothing of working sixteen, seventeen hours a day and my typing reflected these long hours.

My mother would ring me up and ask, helpfully, "Aren't you finished yet?" Friends asked, "What are you doing?" I told them. They replied, "Still?" None of this made me feel any more optimistic. Finally, on December 31, 1977, the very day ordained in my contract for completion, I sent off the revised manuscript – 400 pages, grey. I heaved a sigh of relief and went off for a New Year holiday, convinced that all was over.

I was wrong. My editor came to London three months later. I met him for a drink and to my horror he pulled out of his case my 400 sheets. I was stunned. The copy-editor had gone over my revised words and had some clear ideas about improvements, like abandoning all footnotes and removing some pages, the very pages that had taken me months to write. The blue pencil had been everywhere. My publisher would be in town for five days. "Could you approve each one of these corrections, and NOT IN INK!" I saw my book becoming the copy-editor's. I could not believe that I had to read the whole thing again, and justify myself. I was insulted, but I did it.

The grey sheets went back to New York. And they came back again. Would I redo *all* the source notes, and quickly? I plodded through the same territory again. Everything in quotation had to be identified, even though it had been identified in the text. I thought it was a cruel joke. Double citations struck me as a form of lunacy. I wanted a readable book, not an academic minefield, planted with notes and show-off stuff. Again I gave way.

Proofs finally arrived in May 1978. The covering letter asked me to correct them "as soon as possible" since publication was set for October. I turned to the title page and noticed with considerable alarm that my name had been misspelled – Owen, not Olson. More humiliation. Bound proofs had been sent out to reviewers with the wrong name on the cover. This really was too much.

But I met the deadline. Things were operating to schedule. Then the *New York Times* went on strike, and stayed on strike. Both my agent and publisher agreed that the book ought to be postponed. It was the sort of book that needed reviews and especially a review in the *New York Times Book Review*. It was put back a month. Then it was put back again. Then there was a hold-up at the printers. A new publication date was decided

– January 1979, which meant a new copyright page. Another hold-up.

Finally, in December 1978, the finished copy reached me. It was all over. My excitement had swiftly turned to dread with the finished object in front of me. My friends could walk into any bookshop and see it, buy it. It was no longer mine. It was public. And it was petrifying. My one overriding feeling was utter disbelief, made patently manifest when I walked down Fifth Avenue and saw it in several bookshops. My book. I still don't believe it.

Stanley felt such enormous self-doubt about this project, and Elinor and her relatives so got him down, that if Elinor had not died young (she had a fatal stroke at forty-one) her equally short-lived biographer might not have survived to chronicle a longer career. "Please don't lose heart over your Elinor project – leave that to me," he wrote to editor/publisher James O'Shea Wade, when two years had passed and Chapter Two was yet to be delivered. "I am allowed to hover between depression and suicide about the damn thing; your job is purely Gerhardian – to wait."

And the freakish difficulties Stanley encountered in actually bringing out the book once it was finished go a long way to explain the prepublication hysteria that afflicted him ever afterward. Until the reviews appeared, he was a psychosomatic basket case. Insomnia, "an appallingly regular feature of my life," now became unendurable; he was listening to Wagner till five or six in the morning: "I would like some scorcher variety sleepers. Real snooze anchors," he wrote to his sister.

Asthma, too, had become a feature of his life, though not since its onset in 1971 had he suffered attacks severe enough to disrupt a Sunday walk, as happened with Robert Kee a month before *Elinor*'s publication. "What a departure!" he wrote to Robert. "Heavens, I do apologise for such advanced melodrama. I should have had my medicine with me. I now have 2 extra lots of it so I shall never be without . . ." Six weeks later he felt quite different, he told Robert: "Largely because my violent near-neurotic fits of worry over my book have been allayed, thanks to a host of brilliant reviews, my health is much improved. Aren't nerves a terrible thing?"

The reviews, if not quite "brilliant," were far more complimentary to the biographer than to "the horror of his central subject,"[16] and were certainly favorable enough to justify Stanley's lifted spirits and encourage a further career. "A finely written biography," Grace Schulman said in the *New York Times Book Review*, while lamenting his failure to "create an impressive image" of Elinor. And Avis Berman, in the *Baltimore Sun*, wrote: "Olson's instinct for exploring the recesses of character is admirable, his commitment to telling the truth is all too solid. It will be interesting to contemplate his future as biographer when he has a subject he does not loathe."[17]

Although the book was well and widely reviewed, Dial Press reported scant sales; *Elinor Wylie: A Life Apart* never came out in paperback or in a UK edition. "Stanley's book always seemed rather foredoomed to me by its subject. I didn't think it was a wide enough one for a first biography," says Frances Partridge, who had helped to prune, tidy, and smooth the unruly prose of his early drafts. Even after her labors in London, Jim Wade had his work cut out for him in New York: "I return your draft chapter," he wrote to Stanley, "bleeding slightly from several pores. I know that Elinor can be irritating but I pray you do not let her push you into extremes of archness. Why do you whip your adjectives on to such transports?" When Stanley ranted about his contretemps with the Wylie relatives, Jim responded in a style so like Stanley's that it's no wonder they became great friends: "You must be a psychologist and dim the radiance of your glare under the bland guise of diplomacy (which grosser shepherds know as smarm)."[18]

James Wade and Stanley practiced the now nearly lost art of

editor-author letter writing, and developed a close and lasting friendship based largely upon it. Wit and wisdom, gossip and cajolery crossed the Atlantic frequently, the friends themselves only rarely. Their correspondence – beyond its focus on the flaws and attributes of the manuscript – ranged from the heights of London social life to the depths of New York subway strikes, from Stanley's spaniel to the sleeping habits of the Wade family dog. It was a rare relationship; few editors would spend the time, few authors would inspire the affection.

Stanley's letters were so delightfully funny and astute, his epistolary voice so distinctive and memorable, that his correspondents could easily forget or fail to comprehend his difficulty with book-writing. After he became, finally, an "official" author, with his book in the stores and his name in a flurry of reviews, I was curious to see how he reacted to his new status, and to readers both pleased and aggrieved:

April 20, 1979
Dear Phyllis – I've just had a very funny telephone call from the woman who started the edition of Elinor's letters in 1937 and was great friends with Elinor's son and third husband (they were NOT the same person). She was deeply distressed that I had managed, methodically and accurately, to dismantle one of the myths she had been living with for the last 50 years – namely that E was the most beautiful, most talented, most glorious creature that walked the face of the earth. Now only a myth can hold all those lies without toppling over and crushing itself! She was not pleased that I hated E so much – which, I might add, is a detail only women seem to mention (men say I'm too fair to her) – and that is not true. I met E halfway most of the time and gave her the benefit of the doubt all the time. But one cannot make up material, nor can one ignore the sheer enormity of facts. I could not lie, and Elinor did enough, caused enough pain, that I had to give

way to the truth. With all honesty, I cannot imagine anyone else going through the same material and coming up with a significantly different book. Fair? Are facts ever fair? She lied, she was emotionally retarded and she was gravely unhappy.

Please forgive that spleen-letting. I've had nightmares all night about that telephone call. Writing strikes me as a very gentle, and lethargically slow, form of suicide; otherwise why would one mind such a telephone call? At least she read the book (didn't buy it, I must own; see how conventional we all are when it comes to money?), and had her own sound judgements to make. I suppose all I wanted to hear, after five years' work, was praise. Never mind. That is the test of the professional.

"Some work manages to get sandwiched in between these wild flights from it," Stanley wrote, in April 1979. "The problem is that I am not enjoying it."

An understatement to be sure. The "work" was a one-volume edition of *The Letters and Diaries of Harold Nicolson*, an editing and condensing project he had undertaken, with some misgivings, a few months earlier. The "wild flight from it" was a mad plan he was laying to visit the American South in the dog-days of August. "Longing to see the plants," he said, a desire for subtropical horticulture suddenly overwhelming his notorious loathing of heat and humidity. But he needed a fantasy to sustain him through a bruising work experience, and a vision of lush Spanish moss dripping from antebellum live-oak trees served the purpose for a while; he never actually made the trip.

It all started when *Elinor* was finally in the bookstores, in January 1979, and Stanley found himself out of work. In a letter to Robert Kee he weighed the pros and cons of the only employment prospect on the horizon:

I wanted to ask you about a new job Frances [Partridge]

more or less got for me: editor of Harold Nicolson's Diaries – that is, boiling down the current three [published] volumes and incorporating new material into one huge volume. The points in its favour are 1) it is a job 2) it will give me some money which I sorely need 3) it should only take a year, but a year of full-time work, that is 4) it gives me a toe-hold in the more recent part of this century. Its disadvantages are simply that it hedges my options on anything coming from *Elinor* and will keep me from doing any side work. The case is very much in its favour, but I don't know if it's progress. That is the only thing that holds me back. I am to see Nigel Nicolson next Sunday and will discover more drawbacks no doubt.

Though Robert didn't take seriously Stanley's point about needing money ("One never really believed him about that because he always carried on in such a splendid way"), he did lend him moral and intellectual support while he sorted out the serious career issues confronting him. A few weeks later, Stanley wrote:

As you were informed of the violent indecision over the Harold Nicolson, it is only just that you should be equally informed about its more or less happy resolution. That is a Jamesian way of saying I have been selected as the editor and it is about to begin.

Nigel Nicolson, son of Sir Harold (and Vita Sackville-West), had edited the previous collection of his father's writings, and it is not hard to imagine that blood-ties and possessiveness might have clouded his relationship with *any* subsequent editor. Nevertheless, Stanley got the impression that Nigel had treated him like a hired clerk, and a none-too-competent one at that. When the year was up, he wished to obliterate it from memory. He hated the book and everything connected with it.

Self-interest and discretion dictated that he not talk about these feelings with friends – after all, Nigel Nicolson was

an important man, friend to several of Stanley's friends –
but wounded pride and anger lay close to the surface, even
three years after the book's publication, and prompted an out-
burst of temper in his diary:

> Nigel told Mrs. B. [who had been to a dinner party at
> Sissinghurst recently] that my work on his father's diary
> was slovenly. Now this angered me rather a lot because
> such errors as there were in my typescript were duplications
> of Harold's mistakes. As the publishers wanted a precise note
> made of new entries, I assumed precision was the object.

He then unleashed a stream of vituperative adjectives –
"loathsome," "vile," "despicable," – that better describe his
own feelings of insecurity and defensiveness than they do
Nigel Nicolson, and which had, one hopes, the salutary
effect of "spleen-letting."

What was to be the next project? "After Miss Wylie and Sir
Harold Nicolson K.C.V.O., I think I am well-equipped to
know what it is to spend days of terror and anguish," Stanley
wrote. He told Jim Wade that he was considering Carl Van
Vechten as his next subject. Jim was less than enthusiastic:
"EW had some champagne to her, albeit *très sec et amer*, but
Carlo makes for small beer or, at best, Babycham I think."
There was talk of Lord Duveen and a few other potential
subjects, but nothing seemed to click.

The felicitous pairing of Stanley and J. S. Sargent (expatriate
American painter, 1856–1925) came about with the help of
another "JSS," John Saumarez Smith, who runs the bookshop
in Mayfair where Stanley was a regular (and favorite) customer. "G. Heywood Hill Ltd, Old and New Books" was just

the sort of shop to appeal to him – more like a well-appointed private house belonging to an omnivorous reader than a retail establishment. And John Saumarez Smith was more like a literary consultant than a bookseller. "He knows everybody," says Selina Hastings. "Everyone who is writing books is somehow connected to him. If you are a biographer and want a subject, you consult John first, then a publisher."

Stanley did just that. At lunch one spring day in 1979 he broached the idea of doing a book on the society painter who served, he later said, as "court reporter on the Edwardian Age"; true to form, John was well acquainted with Richard Ormond, deputy director of the National Portrait Gallery and Sargent's grand-nephew and holder of the Sargent copyright. (He also knew that Ormond's own pictorial biography of Sargent was out of print, and that no other good book about the painter existed.)

With the path now smoothed for him by John Saumarez Smith, Stanley approached Richard Ormond who quickly responded to his "infectious enthusiasm" and "insatiable appetite for information," and gave him his blessing, his knowledge, and a great deal of his time: "For six years I was closely involved in the genesis and writing of what, for me, is far and away the most penetrating portrait of J S Sargent ever written. . . . we carried on an extended weekly dialogue that covered every aspect of the painter and his world."[19]

There would be no struggles with *this* subject's relatives: "No one could have a better collaborator," wrote Stanley in his diary, "Richard Ormond is kindness itself." (In gratitude he dedicated the book to him and his wife, Leonée.)

Everything boded well for the success of the project. In short order he acquired a publisher (Macmillan), signed a contract, and secured a Guggenheim fellowship (a feather in his scholar's cap, and a tidy sum in his bank account) to help with travel expenses related to the book. But nothing else in the development of *John Singer Sargent: His Portrait* proceeded with any such haste. "He took great delight in going slowly with his books," his agent Gill Coleridge says. "He was so painstaking and diligent, and he felt that taking a long time to write showed that one was striving for perfection. The sort of writers he admired took a long time."[20] Besides, hurrying through the process would ruin the fun – the joyful prospect of years filled with paintings, travel (especially to Sargent sites like Venice, Paris, Madrid and Boston), and the people to be met in connection with them.

Now he had the opportunity to fulfill the promise that reviewers of *Elinor Wylie* had noted, to test his mettle against a subject he not only didn't loathe but whose life he "adored." He poured forth his excitement in a revelatory letter (which began with a complicated excuse for not having written sooner):

> Heavens, what a way to make an apology! I've been reading too much of Mr Henry James. More accurately I have been reading *The Sacred Fount*, which I have to confess revealed little by page 50. By the time I got to 150 I think I knew less than I did by the first third of that amount. When the wonder volume was shut I knew far less than when I opened it. If James were a mathematician he would have defeated the very rudiments of geometry. As it is he defeated all the laws of progress, let alone progression. Still, it is one of the most glorious books I have ever read. Now if you can follow that, you are paying me a great compliment.
>
> So you can see I am preparing to convert Mr Sargent into a true Jamesian figure: all the ingredients are there – no feeling, no love, no vulnerability. Only a deep and strict adherence to Puritan values. It crowded out people and emotion and distilled work as the only true aspect of life. He was safe. He was immune. And, he achieved it so well that he failed to be unhappy. I do simply adore every aspect of his life. His painting, rather like his life, is all surface and no depth: the portraits are so well-painted as to exclude imagination and fantasy – the very aspects of a truly artistic and interpretive character. These, I believe, at the very heart of everything he produced, were lacking. Hence the glorious slick, and quite seductive,

unimpassioned renderings of his portraits.

I see, by what I have written, that I am immediately converting him into something that he might not have been. Still, if anyone were fool enough to believe that biography is not really well-sheltered autobiography, I am quite happy to let them end their days under that very misapprehension. Don't let the secret out. I still cringe that I might have made Elinor into an Olson-figure rather than permitting her to breathe and feel her own highly limited emotions, her own falsely conceived reality and her oblivion to consequences. But I also might not have. The art of biography will never be understood, quite largely because most biographers refuse to see it as any more than sheer dog-work. I take years and years and the chronic uncertainty is very exciting. Sargent is a real challenge. Elinor was a real obstacle![21]

Though he worried about making Wylie into an Olson figure and Sargent into a Jamesian figure, as the work proceeded it was Olson himself who became a Sargent figure: the painter's brush intensified Stanley's color, highlighted his character, gilded his tastes. "I think he spent the major part of his short life trying to find a proper identity," Gill Coleridge says, "and that identity actually came through once he started writing *Sargent*."

He became obsessed with the man, to a greater degree than is usual between biographer and subject. He wanted to be like Sargent, work like him, share his tastes and quirks and disposition. He wanted to know everything there was to know about him, and seemed to love everything he found out. Early on he gave Gill "a tiny little brown-covered notebook on which he'd written in his lovely spidery handwriting, 'Notes for JSS.' I was to carry this around with me in case I came across anything that related to Sargent," she says.

Stanley found in "JSS" a kindred spirit, and he felt both proprietary and protective of him. When he learned that a woman to whom he'd lent his organization plan for *Sargent* was about to adapt it for a book of her own, he was irked more by her violation of his (and Sargent's) impeccable sense of style than by her appropriation of his scheme:

> If [her] biography enjoys the precise construction of Mr Sargent's I will be very angry indeed and tell her as much. That organisation is a "period" one, quite in tune with the structure of Mr Henry James, and Sargent was, to his toes, a Jamesian figure. [Her subject] is not a Jamesian figure. She must devise some suiting that will fit him, not Sargent's thick tweeds.[22]

On a research trip to Venice he took up watercolors, so he would know how it felt to paint. "My word it is difficult. I don't know how Sargent managed. But I am determined to stick with it." And so he did, with results that occasionally pleased even him. While a guest at Chatsworth, he "painted one moderately decent water-colour and another of quite unbridled awfulness. The people's comments were worth hearing, however, even if I did make a jumbo fool of myself." He started giving watercolor kits as gifts to friends.

Ironically, research into the life of John Singer Sargent – a relentless worker, awesomely prolific – tempted Stanley away from work and toward countless sybaritic distractions, to which he succumbed often, in great style and at considerable cost to his productivity, his pocketbook, and eventually his health. He became grander, more old-fashioned and extravagant with each passing year. Immersion in Sargent's elegant milieu during working hours sharpened his appetite for grandeur the rest of the time. What he called his "luxury necessity" became in fact an addiction, but one which he elevated to an art form. Friends now talked of "Olson of Claridge's" in the way Parisians once spoke of "Proust of the Ritz"; the hotel became his second home, his favored venue for indulging himself and friends. He grew fatter; like Sargent he had a "prodigious appetite that he found difficult to satisfy and one which left his fellow-diners . . . breathless in amazement."[23]

He became a frequent visitor at London's most elegant and expensive shops, especially Asprey's in Bond Street, where the sales assistants adored him and not just because he earned them good commissions on his purchases. He took an interest in them personally, learned from them, amused them. They saw a delightfully Edwardian young-old man – beautifully mannered, obsessed with finery and good living, a stickler for old-fashioned quality.

He redecorated his flat, replacing the handpainted "Bloomsbury" fireplace he had commissioned from Angelica Garnett with a marble one more compatible with his newly acquired French Empire furniture, Sargent's favorite style. He, too, loved its "sturdy elegance. Beauty and stamina, that is what JSS needed to aim for, and Empire satisfied him in it." Stanley's *pièce de résistance* was a bookcase cabinet "of fairly dangerous beauty" (he had to sell off a French chair or two in order to buy it from the Rebecca West estate) that had once belonged to Colonel Swettenham, a colonial governor whose portrait Sargent had painted.

* * *

As Stanley was the first to admit (sometimes boastfully) he took "years and years" to prepare his biographies. No element of the research process received less than scrupulous attention, and the design of a notetaking plan – most crucial element of all – could take months. *Elinor* had taught him the perils of mismanaging records; now he wanted to devise "a crack filing system for Sargent," one that was "fool(me)-proof." "The best I can come up with," he told Robert Kee, "is a three-layer affair (not cake) consisting of . . ." and he outlined an elaborate cross-referenced index-card scheme (which eventually became so refined, it served as a model for other writers). "Oh dear, I can see all my time will be spent being able to locate material rather than doing anything with it."[24]

Indeed, his blend of fussiness and thoroughness made "doing anything with it" a markedly slow-paced affair. He pursued even tenuous leads to an erstwhile owner of a Sargent canvas, sending enquiring letters around the globe. He did not hesitate to spend weeks sorting through passenger lists to track down Sargent's parents' arrival in Liverpool – the ship, the exact time and date. And, of course, he had no truck with modern-day machinery meant to speed a writer's labors. "Though my new electric typewriter is everything I claimed I thought I wanted, I've gone back to the old manual one. Can't bear the noise or the speed, or the ease. The feel is wrong. Such refinement makes me slightly bilious."[25] Word processors were beyond the pale: "appalling devices – cold, bulky and unattractive – and I could never figure out how to work them."

He wrote *Sargent* by hand, in a series of small copybooks, using specially diluted Webster's blue ink in his fountain pens ("Royal blue has too much yellow in it"). Then he typed his drafts on custom-made paper in his favorite color, medium grey. Not only did the odd color necessitate his making carbons (since it photocopied poorly), each sheet had to be cut to size by him. He hired a typing service to produce the fair copy.

One reason for his slowness with *Sargent*, having nothing to do with his eccentric methods but perhaps a great deal to do with the success of the final product, was that Stanley had no formal credentials in art history. He approached Sargent's work – as he did all painting – with an independent mind, a passionate spirit, and a fresh eye. ("I want to go to Prague and look at pictures – an enormous delight to me now," he had written his sister eight years before. "I never thought paintings could be pleasure, but when I went to the Neo-classic exhibition I was there for 4 hours transported by pictures I do not really find excellent, but it was the new way of looking at them that overjoyed me.") Even though his aim in the Sargent biography was "to bring the man out from under the art scholarship," he felt "the hot sinister breath of the art historians on my neck." If he were going to trespass in their territory he had better know exactly where he was headed, and weigh carefully his every step.

> Thought it was about time I came to grips with trying to discuss Sargent's painting. Once I unearthed the fact obvious to others – that painters set out, like writers, to solve certain problems in pictures – it was smooth sailing, because Sargent's American pictures struggled to solve the problem of perspective. So that was one major hurdle leapt, though not deftly vaulted, but I sighed relief. The euphoria of subtly negotiating an intellectual issue is intense and calming – like taking all the wrinkles out of a piece of cloth.[26]

But there were other issues confronting him as biographer of Sargent that taxed his powers and patience more severely. For one: "Sargent said almost nothing about himself or his work, and wrote even less." For another (and certainly unlike anything he had faced with Elinor Wylie):

> Sargent had no private life, no private life in the modern sense of the phrase. And while this never worried *him*, everyone I spoke to seemed unnaturally vexed by the absence of all horizontal activities. This was the most trying issue, and a painful example of our inability to understand the past.[27]

Stanley himself was "unnaturally vexed" by everyone else's vexation. "He became absolutely infuriated if anyone even hinted that a man like Sargent, who worked all the time and had no affairs, no sex life, might be boring," says Gill Coleridge. When Selina Hastings asked him how he planned to handle this sensitive subject in his book, he replied: "I'm not. Why should I? If Sargent didn't like milk chocolate I wouldn't devote a whole chapter to Sargent's not liking milk chocolate."[28]

Friends couldn't help feeling that Stanley's extreme sensitivity and defensiveness on the subject of Sargent's sexuality had its source in his own private life, about which they were for the most part uninformed and curious. "They quickly gave it up as a vacant topic," Stanley wrote, about the ruminations of Sargent's friends (while perhaps suggesting that his own friends should do the same).[29] "As far as sex was concerned, [Sargent] 'just wasn't interested.' "[30]

In reaching his conclusions about this "most trying issue," Stanley had, of course, exercised his customary thoroughness and followed every possible lead. He queried Leon Edel, Henry James's biographer, as to whether there was evidence of a sexual relationship between James and Sargent, whom James had "mesmerized" into moving to London. Edel had uncovered no such evidence. When a scholar "doing work on homosexuality and painters" came to Stanley for data, "I could not help at all," Stanley wrote, "for there is little to no *proof*." He discussed his quandary with Frances Partridge, who responded: "Surely [Sargent] could, in theory at least, have been attracted by men only and been (marginally) inactive. . . . But since when all is said and done human emotions towards each other are more subtle, complicated and interesting than what they do in bed, surely there is room for lots of discovery and interpretation."[31]

Stanley explained Sargent's "absence of intimacy," his preference for "chaste friendship" over sexual love, as stemming from enormous fear at "even the possibility of losing control." "Though willing to take on difficulties in painting, he shirked any such vulnerability in his human relations." He settled instead for "the unthreatening feminine influence" of his devoted sister and older, married women.

In making his case for Sargent, Stanley might just as well have been writing about himself. "I loathe confessions or any approach at intimacy, and still I loathe loathing the omission," he wrote in his diary, at a dark time in his life. He envied Sargent's ability to lose himself so completely in his work, envied his emotional equilibrium and apparent indifference to the absence of intimacy. Stanley could neither work so unremittingly nor absent himself so wholly from the pressures of affection – his own for others and theirs for him. He suffered under the strain of keeping up warm relations with a large number of people while having no one (not even his faraway sister, now married) with whom he could completely relax his guard. It wore him down. "There were those sighs, those deep sighs," says Frances Partridge, of all his friends perhaps the one most aware of his inner turmoil.

> The reaction to Sargent ['s sexuality] sickens me, and that's a fact. Why can't people like the fact he was happy, was an agreeable man? What's all this mad urge for incident? Real artists want a clear run for work, and Sargent achieved it, perhaps at some cost.[32]

If Sargent himself was a paragon of virtue, threatening to bore readers with his hard-working, celibate good-naturedness, there were a host of subsidiary figures in JSS's life whom Stanley could use to seize and sustain readers' attention. Honing his pen nib to an exquisite sharpness, he etched delightfully wicked word-portraits of scores of Sargent's models, colleagues, family members and friends, none more incisive than this sketch of Violet Paget (*nom de plume* "Vernon Lee"):

> Violet threw herself at her books with overburdened conviction; she insisted that learning be the warmth and affection denied her. If anyone ever wore blue stockings, Violet Paget put on two pairs. She turned herself into one of the best-educated and most severely intellectual figures of her day – and one of the most obnoxious, in French, Italian or English. She had a talent for emptying rooms, a real gift

for making enemies and very little ability in keeping friends, and all because she wanted attention. She was, quite simply, too eager or too desperate (or both) for her own good. . . . Her appearance was not much of an asset either: she looked a sleek rodent, eyes glistening, nose twitching, hot on the trail of some tantalizing aroma, impatient and utterly single-minded. She produced some thirty books, a mountain range of fiction, philosophy, criticism, history, aesthetics – indeed, nothing was safe from her attack – all tremendously high-minded, long-winded, respected and now undusted on library shelves.[33]

Jim Wade hoped to publish the American edition of *Sargent*: "I write to enquire, ever so gently, as to the gestation of la vida de JSS? I presume it moves ahead, albeit slowly. It was a life rather more extensive than EW's, so I plan to edit it in a nursing home." As it happened, Jim changed publishing houses and was unable to persuade the new house to take on the Sargent project. Stanley was devastated; he took refuge in his diary.

(Jan. 10, 1983) At 5 Gill [Coleridge] rang me up to tell me she had got no offer whatsoever for Sargent in NY: a lot of flat "no"s – I was amazed; shocked and *very* lowered. I felt, above the standard carry-on about being a failure, that Sargent was insulted. If a subject sells a bio. then they didn't want him. Or wanted him but when they saw my version of him they wanted him no more. Quite frankly I am perplexed. I will plod on, and pray someone in NY feels like backing me. Altogether I feel shop-soiled and a future failure.

(Feb. 3, 1983) How fragile our moods are – the post brought a very decent letter from New York giving the run-down on poor Sargent's future with potential publishers. The issues were set out clearly and a huge attempt had been made to offer encouragement, but all I read was failure and misery.

In the park I started to concoct my reasons for shelving the whole book. Then Gill rang and said some offers had in fact been made and some high notes of admiration had been sounded – the whole effect was that one was radically changed – lifted, renewed, and everything greatly improved, greatly. Oh, perhaps I must learn to live with the fact I am no better than second rate, and it is an undeniable fact, but for one moment I was able to forget it. Perhaps that is all we ever try to do: forget the awfulness of life.

His flair for splendid self-indulgence was a great aid in forgetting ("I've a real weakness for Taxi deliveries, among other luxes," he told a friend whose quiet Christmas was disturbed when a cabdriver came to her door bearing a gift from Stanley for her dog), but the cascade of bills that followed in its wake and splashed across his desk served as a depressing reminder. "My attitude towards money is so awful and strange I even shock myself," he confessed to his diary. Though his financial statements showed an investment portfolio paying good dividends, he was living largely on credit and felt "poor as they come and dead broke. I suppose I equate money to success, and as I earn none I am a failure." At such times, even "gentle chidings" from his father for "messing about with my accounts again" were enough to make him wrench his phone from the wall.

(Feb. 20, 1983) Feel v. shaky, v. despondent, useless, etc. All the old stuff again. Work very hard to counteract growing sense of despair. . . . It seems moods are abated only by work, but if moods are grave how can there be work?

(Feb. 16, 1983) Perhaps all this mood talk merits some discussion. I feel, no believe, I am a failure and that at all turnings in what passes for my career, I have taken the wrong one – and have not been able to recoup.

The mood of despair was not helped by the fact that

his friend Rebecca West was slowly and painfully dying.

"Stanley always looked terrible when he was depressed. Very pasty. His skin went dull, puffy," says Selina Hastings. "And sometimes he'd be rather silent, but we'd make him laugh and he'd be all right." Artist Susannah Phillips, who had done his portrait, was shocked to see how different he looked at such times – "pale and blubbery, like a great white whale." Friends tried to coddle him out of his moods, sending messengers with champagne or sweets, ploys which usually worked. But when "moods" gave way to deep depression, as they did, off and on, during the winter of 1982–83, he ignored the phone, let no one in, and went outdoors only to walk the dog. His self-esteem plummeted to the point where he felt an "utter loathing of people's affection for me."

Then spring arrived and, along with a cheering crop of white flowers in the mews courtyard, good news: St. Martin's Press would publish the American edition of *Sargent*, and editor Joyce Engelson, a straight-talking, kindhearted New Yorker, pledged her staunch support. She liked what she'd seen of his draft, and when they met in person, in London, she thought he was "darling. Absolutely unique. The consummate English gentleman – except for his dearness. There is nothing dear about a *real* English gentleman."[34]

She knew London literary and social circles well enough to be impressed when he told her stories about the people and places he knew. "But it wasn't showing off or name-dropping. He was sharing – telling me things that he knew would amuse me. . . . And the way he could eat!" Of course he selected a superbly elegant restaurant for their expense-account dinner, and complied bounteously when asked to order for both of them. "It was marvellous food, but every course, from appetizer to dessert, had cream in it. 'What is it with this guy and cream sauce?' I wondered." (Even Stanley found it too rich: "feeling unwell," he noted in his diary next day.) "And when he took me down to his wonderful work space in the mews, and showed me all his Sargent notes and files,

I thought: 'My god, this is an enterprise. He has more stuff on Sargent than Sargent had on Sargent. But there's so little *done* on this book. He's never going to get it done.'"

Macmillan's editors worried, too, when after nearly three years of work and within a couple of months of the completion date stipulated in the contract, less than a third of the book was written "and then only in a very preliminary draft" form. Gill Coleridge negotiated a contract extension, and Stanley somehow pulled himself over the hump; from then on the pace of work quickened. Years later, when the book came out and a friend commented on "a shift in tone, an opening up" that seemed to occur about a third of the way into it, he replied: "There is an odd reason for this, and it is none too thrilling. I wrote and rewrote the first five sections of the book over too long a time and with too much intensity. Fear – and I was very frightened of what I had taken on – does odd things to a narrative."[35]

"The build-up to the great crisis of publication" began in 1985, his sixth and final year of writing *Sargent*. "He was in a perpetual tizz, anxious and frustrated. Of all the many authors I've represented," Gill Coleridge says, affection and concern for him still inflecting her voice, "Stanley was the one who got himself into the greatest state of anxiety about book publication."

It also happened that he experienced an unusual number and variety of difficulties in the process. Once he had finally finished the writing and rewriting ("I can safely say, scarcely one word has been left untormented"), he was adamant that the printed book be ready for the opening of two major Sargent exhibitions in New York – at the Coe Kerr Gallery, in May 1986, and the Whitney Museum in October. But as late as spring 1985, his two publishers had not yet decided whether there would be two separate editions – one British and one American, reflecting their different editorial and design preferences (and further complicating his life) – or one "common" edition, which would reduce editorial and production costs and speed the book's release (but require a great deal of coordination between them). Eventually they decided on the latter: Macmillan would handle production, St. Martin's would print from Macmillan's plates, and each would do their own book jacket. Needless to say, coordination was the sticking point in this arrangement, with Stanley caught in the middle.

(March 28) Mounting fury at those nincompoops. Publishers. They lie – all the time.

(March 29) Macmillan & St Martins have been going 40 rounds and there is no victor and neither seems to have been in the fight at all. At least neither know what they have been doing in the ring. Phones broken at Gill's office. I give up – entirely.

(March 30) More of the same – in bed all day. Refuse to answer phone.

He had already lost two Macmillan editors when, suddenly, just as *Sargent* entered its final phase, Joyce Engelson left St. Martin's. "The world very nearly collapsed," Gill Coleridge says. On top of all this, Stanley was threatened with a plagiary lawsuit by a man he knew to be "a reflex litigant," but one who had dogged other Sargent writers to near-suicide. He worried that his publishers' lawyers, who had contractual responsibility for defending him in such matters, might underestimate this threat and do nothing, or else overreact and postpone or cancel publication.

"I feel as if it might be right to suffer from persecution mania," he wrote. "Felt dreadfully unwell at the London Library and had to get a reviving glass of champagne which did [revive]. Then another at Claridges which made me feel so well, I was unwell."

When things finally progressed to the design stage, Stanley drove the book-production people on both sides of the Atlantic "absolutely potty." (He wanted neither blurbs nor photograph of himself on the cover – "I am very against quotations on the jacket, very against. Nothing puts my back up more than being told what to think about the contents of a book.") Yet he did it so politely, with such wit and grace that they rarely held it against him. ("I look forward to meeting you and everyone else who has been victimised by me at St Martins," he wrote to an editorial assistant in New York, after admitting somewhat disingenuously that his fears and fussiness were founded more on "distance and ignorance" than on reason.)

"Strange how I've no feeling whatever about having finished Sargent. None." The diary entry of a battle-fatigued, shell-shocked writer, too long in the trenches. But the feeling-vacuum soon filled. On one of his specially printed postcards announcing Macmillan's upcoming (April 10, 1986) publication of *John Singer Sargent: His Portrait*, Stanley wrote: "It only bores me now, and covers me with shame. I want to rewrite the WHOLE thing, so convinced am I it is worse than bad. At least when the reviews appear, I can agree with them with sincerity." His signature – a nearly invisible squiggle, much tinier than usual – mirrored his fear.[36]

Ecstasy displaced anxiety when the great publication day dawned. "It was an *enormous* event for him, a glorious triumph," Gill Coleridge says. Stanley and Sargent held center stage at two parties and in the book review page of the [London] *Times*. The National Portrait Gallery and the Tate Gallery engaged him for lectures. "He was in heaven!" says Frances Partridge.

Since a publisher could hardly be trusted to organize a proper fête, Stanley himself had subtly taken charge of Macmillan's book-launch party, leaving to them only the tasks of mailing invitations to everyone he knew and paying the wine-seller's bill. Months before, he had selected the party site – the Fine Arts Society, in Bond Street: "As it was one of the first galleries to show You-know-who in London in the late 1870's," he wrote Macmillan's, "there is more than a slim connection, and thus [my] fat recommendation that they might be considered" for the party. (That phrase – "might be considered" – typifies Stanley's smooth but sure technique of manipulation. "He could be very determined. There was an iron hand within that velvet glove," says the Duke of Devonshire.)[37]

Stanley's own luncheon party for eighteen, at Claridge's, turned out a perfect success, a masterpiece of planning and *placement* that friends remembered ever after as his shining moment.

Some weeks later, a writer from the fashionable rag *W*, lured by "reviews so contradictory they are the talk of London's literary circuit," called on Stanley at the mews, sipped Perrier-Jouet Rosé while conducting the interview, and then summarized for readers the pronouncements of the British press:

> *The Times* of London [James Fenton] said the book was so good it should win a prize. *The Observer* [Hilary Spurling] said it read as if it had been written by a computer with cloth ears. However, a second *Observer* writer [Cynthia Kee] said, "To read is to see, is what I felt when I put down the book," and *The Sunday Times* [Andrew Sinclair] said, "Olson makes a silk prose out of a sorry subject; aphorisms and illuminating insights embellish this account of a dull routine."[38]

Stanley himself felt "tremendous delight" in what *he* took to be the reviewers' general "uniformity" of opinion about his book; they agreed, more or less, with *Irish Times* reviewer Terence de Vere White's assessment that it was "an eccentrically brilliant performance." And as for the problem of JSS's "lack of horizontal activities":

> One review did gratify me the most – from *Gay Times* – as here was the one quarter which had a vested interest in having Sargent enrolled into the Lavender Mafia and was so impressed by my account of his life, there was no sorrow in his not being able to join.[39]

But what would they say about Sargent on the *other* side of the Atlantic? No sooner had the afterglow of April 10 worn off than Stanley's frenzy about June publication in America set in. He was not encouraged by what he saw of the book in New York in May, when he went to the Coe Kerr Gallery show. The illustrations had not fared well in the offset process; photographs of Sargent paintings were intolerably dim, diagrams were in the wrong place, and:

> for every error I corrected in proof, they made another in the final printing. Poor as the English edition is, the American one is miles worse, which is why I will not have a copy on my shelves. I sent back my free copies. Can't bear to look at it.[40]

On the other hand, he loved the dust jacket on the American edition: "VERY VERY VERY HANDSOME," he exclaimed to a St. Martin's editorial assistant. "There is not the slightest hint of anything but real excellence about it. Could you please send me the name of the designer so I might thank them/him/her directly?" If only the British edition had such a marvelous cover, he said.

Nothing could please him altogether; he played one publisher against the other because he was terrified and insecure about the entire publishing process, about his career as a writer, about his life on the whole. And because, unknown to everyone, there was an electrical storm brewing in his brain.

In mid-July, when he expected major American reviews to appear, he took to phoning Gill Coleridge three times a day – just in case she had been sent advance copies. He complained to Selina Hastings of "appalling headache," the worst pain he'd ever experienced. One side of his face looked very odd, she said; he *must* go and see his doctor.

By the time most of the American notices appeared that summer, Stanley could no longer read; he was hospitalized and fighting for his life. At least one review – the most influential of all, in the *New York Times Book Review* – would have pleased him exceedingly; its terms of praise were quite similar to those he used himself when he liked a piece of writing: Olson's *Sargent*, Roger Kimball said, has passages that are "witheringly funny," and prose that is "a rich, almost Jamesian affair, ferociously literate, archly elliptical."[41]

Stanley's great friendship with Rebecca West during the last decade of her ninety-year life came about because of *Elinor Wylie*, and was certainly the most profound consequence of his struggles on that book. Pursuing a lead about the acquaintance of West and Wylie in New York in the 1920s, Stanley called on Dame Rebecca in 1974, at her Kensington Gardens flat, and was startled to learn that she not only knew the infamous Elinor well, but "adored her – was perhaps the only person who did."[42]

Always an advocate of the underdog (but with a some-times perverse notion of whom to include in that category), Dame Rebecca was grateful that someone was writing about her old friend – "a figure who has slipped out of sight while her inferiors have been over-remembered"[43] – and willingly supplied the neophyte biographer with firsthand anecdotes about Elinor and many of the secondary figures in her life.

When four years later she reviewed proofs of the finished biography, a battle-scarred Stanley felt his struggles had been rewarded: "She read it, it seems, in one sitting and has written to say it was 'beautiful.' She has recommended some minor adjustments, but they are so small, I feel fairly confident that I have been accurate throughout. ... Praise from Rebecca West is really head-turning."[44]

"Rebecca West lived her life operatically," Victoria Glendinning has written,[45] and no one was more vulnerable to its music than Stanley. Once introduced to it, he determined to hear as much as possible. He pursued Dame Rebecca, he devoted himself to her, and he won over the famous, formidable and mistrustful old woman simply by being himself – that is, exceptionally considerate, intelligent, amusing and generous. His talent for being "The Gazette" no doubt helped; she adored gossip. And if ever he had broached the subject of his ethnic background, that too would have gone over well. Throughout her life she had a soft spot for Jews, identified with them, even looked for one to marry.

He set about reading all of her books and "rattled on about them to everybody."[46] He grew flowers especially for her, and hosted intimate luncheons at his flat to bring her together with Sybille Bedford, Selina Hastings and others of his friends. Rebecca became very fond of him, depended on him. At a party to which he escorted her, "she grew hysterical when he got out of her sight. 'Where's Stanley? Where's Stanley! I'm frightened without him,' " she said to another guest.[47] "He put himself out enormously for her, which was lovely for both of them," says Gill Coleridge, one of the first to whom he boasted of his new conquest. "He was so *proud* of their friendship!"

To Jim Wade in New York he wrote:

London is dusty, vile and hot and I am dining amidst intense grandeur tonight with Dame Rebecca West. I suppose I will dine à la Blanche Knopf, that is, on a lettuce leaf followed

by a lavish portion of air soufflé because it is so hot to-day
...[48] (Wade's response: "I hope you enjoyed your lettuce
leaf chez West. Anyone who can stomach H. G. Wells can
eat anything.")

Stanley regarded Rebecca with an equal measure of admiration and affection, the most potent combination in his
emotional repertoire. And the more he learned about her –
the more he experienced of this astonishingly accomplished
woman who was yet so touchingly vulnerable – the more he
cared for her.

The two spent many an afternoon conversing in her
drawing-room, their talk punctuated by laughter when one
or the other struck just the right note of clever malice. He'd
retail the latest London literary gossip, she'd reminisce about
her adventures in America – fending off publisher Horace
Liveright's advances in a New York taxicab; or being introduced to Charlie Chaplin who promptly invited her to dinner
and bed, and then sent a letter telling her he couldn't face it.
(" 'Of course I had no intention of going to bed with him,
but it was an extraordinary thing to be told.' ")[49]

A connoisseur of biting ripostes, Stanley copied into his
diary a few choice examples from Rebecca's conversation.
To a man with "a terrible willingness to be a guest," she had
said – "Thank you for coming; it was extremely kind of you,
especially as you are so busy, and as you were not asked." She
talked about someone's "instinct for failure," which struck
Stanley as "a phrase painfully applicable to many people of
my acquaintance – perhaps even me."

During "the drawn-out enterprise" of Rebecca's final illness and death, Stanley, too, went into decline. "I feel the
indignity inflicted on RW very much and I mind dreadfully,"
he wrote when a hired nurse took photos of Rebecca in the
hospital and entertained in her flat. He "minded" emotionally and viscerally: "Went to the library to try to detonate
my mood and was overcome, like some fast-moving vehicle,

by colossal hunger. This can mean only one thing – nerves."

It was a dreadful time, that winter of 1982–83. His chief protagonists, two of the pivotal characters in his life, were suffering – Rebecca buffeted by pain in London, Sargent by rejection in New York – and he was helpless to alleviate it. He drank, ate, and drugged himself to excess, slept little, worked fitfully.

> Such an odd dream early this morning. I dreamt I had suffered a stroke and was having luncheon at a house owned by perfect strangers. I saw an object moving in the corner of the dining room which turns out to be a smooth-haired cat. Wuzzo starts to take some interest and I pick up the cat to protect him (Wuzzo). The cat sinks his claws into me and I can again not move – though I had enough mobility to get the cat. My host motions for no one to rescue me from the mauling cat. When after some time the cat is unpicked from my skin, I lift my mobile hand and see five v. deep, v. deep wounds that do not bleed at all.

He maintained daily contact with Rebecca's devoted house-keeper Tessa Monro, but otherwise retreated from social life and frequently disconnected his phone. During this period of unprecedented inwardness, he wrote often in his diary, using it, as he never had before, to examine "the whole tidal process of these emotions." A decade earlier he had worried about outliving his closest friends; now for the first time he confronted that prospect.

> (Dec. 9, 1982) Just back from seeing RW: very frail, looking not at all well, but her flashes of brilliance still there. On speaking about our friendship: "Mutual esteem and malice towards all."

> (Jan. 11, 1983) Some, but oh so little heartening news: I have been asked to talk about RW on the radio; then, after being cheered I was uncheered, for I felt that I was trading

on Rebecca's friendship, using her. I will have to point out to the Radio man that I have these feelings and he must measure my comments by that rule.

(Feb. 7, 1983) Went to visit Mrs Monro . . . read a wonderful essay by Rebecca on the Englishman abroad. She writes like an angel, is a deft and ready scholar and has perfect control over every sentence. Mrs M was in a lowish mood. This drawn-out enterprise of RW's death is beginning to tell on everyone, and there is probably little hope that it will come soon, which I pray it will.

(Feb. 12, 1983) All day I was menaced by a fury over the state of Rebecca: while I miss her and for all purposes she is dead, she is tortured endlessly and in ways we simply can't imagine. I can't stop thinking about her.

(March 2, 1983) This time last year I took RW some daffodils which I grew – white, very pretty – and she was very pleased. She loved them.

(March 10, 1983) Rebecca's health has taken a sharp decline: pneumonia in one lung; she takes short shallow breaths; she is obliged to sleep on one side. It looks to [be] the end in a few days. Let us pray it is.

(March 12, 1983) Cancel [trip] because Mrs M[onro] has asked me to stay in town in case . . . I stay in town by means of staying in bed all day . . . Very poor show on my part, but in truth I am gravely depressed, which is expressed by means of eating constantly and making what had been pure fatigue as my excuse, positive unwellness by excess all round. Oh dear, feel most awfully odd. Speak to Mrs M about 3 or 4 times. RW holds on, somehow. And as we miss her now, what will it be like?

Then on March 15, 1983:

I have waited for this day, for the shift of verb tense,

longing for RW to end her torture – a preparation one would have thought buttressed me from sadness. Well, it has not worked. I am very sad, and for the very reasons totally unattached to reason. She was really too great for us. Also, she was singular to a degree unknown. She possessed an odd variety of gyroscope inside, with the magnetic poles somehow misaligned so as to make everything that seemed in order to be not so. North was not quite north and yet she was able to convince you it had every reason not to be altogether north. She brought the gifts of fiction to nonfiction and vice versa. But most of all she was a wonderful person. I loved her – yes, that is it. I considered her to be my beacon for this idiotic profession. And she was generous to a fault. But all this is flushed from a well of sadness. History will prove her true status in the history of – well, you name it – almost every department: philosophy, history, literature, etc. This is dangerous prediction, but the source of this flare is very profound. Make no mistake, the likes of her has never been seen before and will never be seen again. Oh, how she will be missed by everyone who has anything holding his ears apart. I must adjust the arrangement of my life, for now there is a severe omission in this hopeless sphere.

(Fate possesses an acute sense of the ironic or comic: the serialized book on the World Service at 2:30 a.m. Wednesday [the night after RW's death] was *Ann Veronica* by H.G. Wells. Surely Fortuna smiles in a peculiar way.)

(March 17, 1983) The absurdity of the human condition never ceases to define and explain itself in amazing ways. I went to see Rebecca's body today, Thursday, at a funeral director's place in Westbourne Grove. The part of town was not agreeable. I was extra nervous. I rang the doorbell on the copper plate outside, which had some sort of speaking device [built into it]. Nothing. I rang again. Then some matron stormed to the front in a rage only vaguely concealed. "I heard the bell; I was on the phone!" My nerves did not improve.

She took me through endless halls all decorated in the very worst seaside-hotel taste, with wooden runners halfway up the walls for coffin protection. Through hideous waiting room, up some stairs with unmatching bannisters. Then downstairs to a hideous minute chapel, very cold, with RW in repose in the plain coffin. Open. Covered with some embroidered cloth. She was dressed in a pretty nightdress, blue and white, over which was draped some hideous white satin. Her hands were crossed with a rosary entwined. They were a pale translucent yellow colour and I rather thought they were fake. Her spectacles were round her neck as always and her face was very calm. It was an unbearable sight and I'm ashamed to say I broke down and roared out the place. On the way out, charmless matron was droning into the phone about carpets. Back into that hideous street.

I felt horrid all day. The sight of Rebecca in that awful place was too much. Ninety years of battle, work, dignity had come to a stop inelegantly; the futility of a great life . . .

(March 20, 1983) Rebecca – all that is Rebecca now – lies in that horrid ugly box, her hands yellowing. . . . It strikes me that this is a pretty shoddy culmination of life, and altogether not worthy of her. Grief is very odd. It now comes on me in waves. Mercifully I am so ill-acquainted with the emotion that I remain fascinated by its operation and effect.

Stanley's sojourn in the unfamiliar territory of grief was soon interrupted by news from Rebecca's solicitors that brought him to a more familiar emotional landscape – "the realm of bruised vanity." Dame Rebecca had done an extraordinary thing: on an undated card, but in handwriting from the end of her life, she had authorized not one but *two* biographers and then failed to specify their briefs beyond the fact that Victoria Glendinning was to write the "first" "short" biography and Stanley Olson the "second" "full" one.

If she intended to generate chaos from the grave, she was thoroughly successful. Everyone was baffled by her cryptic designation – her executors, Victoria Glendinning, and especially Stanley. "I thought he was going to throw himself off the bridge," Gill Coleridge says. Years before, he had told her "in absolute confidence" that Rebecca was thinking of naming him as her biographer. "I knew how much he wanted this, but I cautioned him: 'You mustn't set too much on this; it's very unlikely.' He was late in her life, young, an American, a man – all sorts of things that might make him totally unsuitable."[50] But with the passing of time and the deepening of their friendship, Stanley grew increasingly confident. (And with good reason: there was later found among her personal papers a formal statement granting him exclusive access to materials otherwise sealed until her son Anthony's death. The handwriting predated that on the card naming two biographers.)[51]

"It was the most appalling lack of clarity in a will," Gill Coleridge says. "Until the executors and everyone worked out what the extent of Victoria's 'short' book would be, it wasn't possible to know what Stanley's book would include. At first he felt threatened by Victoria, who was much better known than he, and of course he worried that she would skim off the cream; that seemed inevitable, under the circumstances."

"The arrangement is unlivable with," he wrote in his diary,

at least from what one knows on the surface. Is that reaction just vanity shouting or brutal common sense? Perhaps R. spotted my limitations or few strengths (which I agree with, but then again I would) and acted accordingly. It does rather shove me into the backwater of achievement. Like exploring, biography's goal is a continent or mountain, not the catalogue of flora and fauna that follows up.

During the series of meetings and interviews launched by Rebecca's executors to sort out the confusion, Stanley's misery grew palpable. "He felt [the executors] were patronizing him, and it made him angry and it made him cry," says Gill Coleridge, who accompanied him to the sessions and negotiated on his behalf. "And when he was irritated and uptight about things, he could be very spiky."

He had once observed that both Wests (Rebecca and Anthony) tended to see "the spectral workings of villainy behind every corner"; now he too became somewhat paranoid. Every slight, real or imagined, every moment of insecurity – from infancy to Culver to the Nicolson débâcle to his current fears for *Sargent* – came to the fore and plagued him. He may have felt a posthumous anger at Dame Rebecca and displaced it onto her executors; in any case, his contacts with them always rankled, even intensified two years later when they held another series of negotiations about access to Rebecca's papers: (March 29, 1985) "Towering rage all day. The RW thing brews & festers & boils over."

Against all the odds, however, the relationship between Rebecca West's two biographers was a stunning success – in Stanley's case a triumph of good sense over wounded pride, in Victoria's an example of admirable unselfishness. He knew that "the great list of problems supplied by that thin description in the will" could best be resolved by the biographers themselves, and when Victoria (whom he'd met only once, years before) took the initiative toward friendship, he responded totally.

> I told Stanley straightaway that I would share all my material with him; there would be no secrets between us, I was not going to be possessive about Rebecca. And I decided early on to dedicate the book to him, to show that we were in this together, that we were colleagues on a shared project.[52]

With the generosity and helpfulness customary in his dealings with fellow writers, Stanley now offered Victoria the flexibility that Dame Rebecca's bifurcated scheme had seemed to preclude:

> If, after you get to work, you find an intolerable obstacle to your "short" biography, we will put our heads together

and come up with something that might help to reduce that obstacle. ... The only thing which I think is sacred is the biography – short *and* full ... Am I correct in saying (& thinking) we have this easy unrufflable working partnership? The answer is, I know, yes.

When the raw edges of hurt and confusion wore off, his new status appeared to him in a more favorable light. If praise from Rebecca West had been head-turning, then being named her official biographer (even if not solo) put a gold seal on his career. This was the big break, just the sort of "return on investment" he'd been promising his parents for years. (Indeed, when he and Macmillan signed a book contract in 1986, the sum of money to be paid him over a nine-year period was so substantial, "he took it as one of the benchmarks in his life."[53])

Meanwhile he had nearly three years of work on *Sargent* to complete, plenty of time in which to have mixed feelings about the monumental task he faced thereafter: "RW's biography is a prospect that makes my knees quake, and when they are done doing that they turn to jelly. A fine how-do-you-do," he confessed to his diary. And to Victoria Glendinning: "The strain of Rebecca's elbows on Sargent's shoulders is beginning to kill me and not help Sargent. What am I to do?"

If ever his self-doubt went dormant, it clearly reawakened when Victoria had finished her book on Rebecca and he prepared to begin his. His words to her now echoed his diary entry from three years before:

> I could not possibly consider doing *IT* without your having done *IT* first. And though I might have the longer job, you have had/are having the much worse. As you must have seen in Sargent, I am really only good at the fine needle-work and am rotten at looming the cloth.[54]

Although the weight of Rebecca's elbows never quite

lifted from his shoulders, he carried it well in public. In an interview for *London Portrait* magazine about *Sargent*, Louise Roddon asked Stanley about his forthcoming project: "Rebecca will take ages," he said, "and her life is the exact reverse of Sargent. I was constantly having to push him to the front – with her, I'll be saying 'get back!! get back!!' She'll probably be the last." And what would he do then? Roddon asked. He shrugged and chuckled: "Who knows? Die probably!"[55]

Stanley's career as biographer foundered on the great rock of Rebecca West. There was to be no rescue.

PART IV

THE SYBARITE: A HEADLONG
RUSH TO DOOM

People whose lives have been in danger for a long time are always the most extravagant.

Rebecca West, in the film *Reds*

Nothing like a concentrated blast of luxury to convert sour mood to sweet one. I recommend it enormously.

Stanley to Victoria Glendinning, 1968

"Life is rather overrated and puffed up. After all, it is so soon over," Stanley wrote in 1972, after drafting his will. But while it lasted he would live with *carpe diem* as his motto, and a guiding principle that went something like this: "Life is short and unhappy at its core, so let us make the best of it by giving pleasure to ourselves and others." What those who loved him looked upon as surfeit – excessive, gluttonous, "unbridled spoilification," Susan Loppert called it – Stanley saw as essential to a brief sojourn through an otherwise barren life. He lived as if aware that his death might come as prematurely as his birth; in the interval there would be wondrous abundance.

If only there weren't such a problem paying for it. "It is utterly impossible to earn money these days," he wrote Arlene in June 1977, "and with the Budget yesterday [raising the value-added tax rate], Christ how one needs it. I have given up drink and much of the luxe life – this [Claridge's] writing paper apart."

If he intended to arouse his sister's sympathy, he surely dashed it two paragraphs later when describing his birthday dinner at the Connaught: lobster, chateaubriand and strawberries. And his birthday presents if not "luxe" were certainly abundant: "2 books, 3 bottles of champagne, 2 slap-up dinners, 2 doz roses (sneeze), a plant, 17 cards, soap from Herr Drugg [the neighborhood chemist], and 3 birthday cakes."

Whatever his immediate financial situation, it was inconceivable that Stanley own or give less than the best (even when the recipient – his postman, for instance – might actually prefer a fiver to a box of Belgian chocolates at Christmas). "Everything of quality, the essential pleasures, he generally took to," Sybille Bedford says. "And he liked quality because he liked quality; it wasn't because of what other people thought." When a friend injured her leg, he gave her a walking stick – not just an ordinary stick, but an elegant ebony one. When Arlene asked him to arrange a gift for a family friend in London, he organized "a beautiful honeycomb in a Limoges dish, some vintage marmalade in a bone china dish and something else I can't remember. If she doesn't like the honey she will like the dish." When a hostess made him a special cocktail he craved ("It was a nightmare to do. He loved it so much, and we all drank it at the time because he was one of those people who would set the trends and one would do it."[1]), he had Asprey's send her a crystal jug specially designed for mixing and pouring that drink. When his cleaning lady's husband had a fine job prospect, he gave the man one of his custom-made suits and an appointment with his tailor to alter it to his measurements.

When his gifts weren't grand, they were unusually clever or thoughtful: for a man who has everything, like the Duke of Devonshire, a horse-racing enthusiast with the oldest registered colors on the British turf, he hunted down a scarf in the Duke's racing colors, a pale yellow called "straw" on the racing card. For a pregnant friend who suffered even more than he did from the summer heat, he found a purse-size, battery-driven fan that she could take with her everywhere. And since he believed in the maxim "meanness to one's friends is not very pretty, but to be stingy to oneself is despicable,"[2] his largess nearly always extended to a second box of chocolates, a second walking stick or cooling-fan for himself.

In the interest of economy Stanley mixed pleasure with business whenever possible, occasionally managing to persuade others to subsidize his self-indulgence while calling it work. To an editor he knew at *Food & Wine* magazine he wrote (on Claridge's stationery):

> You can see I do not just eat in hotels; I steal. Do you suppose the removal of all writing paper from the desks in the foyer of the Ritz has anything to do with me? I've now side-stepped to Claridge's. By the way, I am about to start on the biography of John Singer Sargent. What tales *that* research will produce. Would you like – I can see you flinch after reading those words; no, of course you wouldn't like, but will listen anyway – an article about eating while researching? Dining with complete strangers as I had to do so often while writing *Elinor*, and staying at such odd places as the Graduates' Club at Yale which housed 9 men none of them, save me (and after three weeks I wasn't so sure), under 85. Whew!

Cunning query letters like this netted Stanley several grand-hotel dinners, from London to Baden-Baden, along with a chance to sample peripheral pleasures between meals: "Baden-Baden was rather spectacular," he wrote his sister. "I took the air and the waters and completely rejuvenated myself. I had a glorious bath in a baroque *chambre* with crystal chandelier and silk furniture. Such grandeur."

Even the octogenarian-filled Yale club could well serve a writer who knew his pleasures and how to capitalize on them. The club had on staff one "Charlie," a bartender who inspired Stanley's article "Why I Am Devoting My Life to Reviving the Cocktail":

> Charlie was a wonderful man with snow-white hair and a pure ivory smile. He was educated on the Pullmans, that forcing-house for alcoholism, and his cocktail repertoire outstripped even the *Savoy Cocktail Book*. During my stay at the Club,

Charlie unveiled the intricacies of his vast knowledge.

His best creation was a Sidecar (cointreau, lemon juice and brandy). He took no short-cuts, apart from having abandoned his jigger-measure. Lemon was freshly squeezed. Ice was cracked for each drink. Glasses were housed in the freezer. And he raised his silver shaker, well dented, high into the air and throttled the life out of the poor mixture. It was smooth, tasting neither of cointreau nor brandy – two of my most detested spirits – nor of lemon juice. It was perfect. Heaven.

It was at the Yale Graduates' Club that I learned the essential rule for cocktail drinking: never change posture. I do not recommend trying to stand or sit after four of Charlie's Torpedo Cocktails (gin, brandy and apple brandy); hammers will start to fall out of the sky and the floor be seen to shift.[3]

And the liver will ache and the waistband rebel. In 1977 when his high living caught up with him, Stanley wrote his parents:

I tried to get into a health farm because I concluded, in my absurd manner of logic, that it was the only answer to the [Christmas] week of enforced bonhomie and gluttony. Well the only fat palace open over Christmas was the grandest one of all, costing, if you please, £315 a week!!! I did not race to make a booking. Really that is absurd when you think how they starve you, beat you, torture you, and charge extra for a dog.

Instead, he told Arlene, he had found a cure closer to home:

I'm on a VERY STRICT diet, and more surprising not miserable about it. I went to the doctor and asked him why my proportions – a discreet term for a region you know of – are billowing out unrestrainedly. He took a blood sample and then said quite calmly: "Bad blood" – which should be taken as no reflexion on you or Them but on too much drink. So drink is totally out, but totally, and it is not missed, either. When I told another doctor of this analysis, he calmly uttered the word "Phooey! There is no such thing as bad blood." Well, the excuse worked for me and I feel much better.

No such excuse weaned him (for more than a day or two) from fattening food, and it's a wonder, under the circumstances, that his proportions didn't "billow" into outright obesity. The time he spent talking about food, planning and eating it was phenomenal; he gave to it a lover's obsessive attention – as if food were love, the giving of love, the receiving of love. Indeed, "his way of making love to me," says Henrietta (Partridge) Garnett, "was to take me for frightfully expensive dinners, with caviare and champagne, which we were supposed to eat in absolute silence." The abstention from conversation while feasting was tacitly understood to be a reverential act, a worshipful homage to the god of food who, in Stanley's pantheon, had displaced the god of love.

Even when he had guests coming but no time to cook, or on the rare occasions when he dined alone at home, the most luxurious food arrived at the mews, pre-prepared, from Le Gavroche and other fine restaurants. Nor did he limit himself to London suppliers; his favorite source abroad was Harry's Bar, and friends returning from vacation in Venice were usually willing to deliver dinner to Stanley on their way home from the airport.

Could there be anyone whose food fixation and exacting standards better qualified him to evaluate purveyors of victuals? Stanley's friend Susan Campbell, editor of *The Guide to Good Food Shops*, thought not; she solicited these comments when preparing her 1979 edition and 1981 update of the guide:

BLAGDEN'S. Just as good, if not better, than before. They are quite willing, if not altogether overjoyed, to deliver ¼ lb.

of smoked salmon, which, I repeat, remains the very best in London. They do, however, overcook their gull's eggs. Guinea fowl perfectly dressed, as are their lobsters. I swear by them.

BARTHOLDI. A must after a hard day at the British Museum. I even saw Lord Annan in there. Perfect staff. One of the few places where you can get real sauerkraut and Westphalian ham and fleischkase. I go there every Friday for weekend food. Perfect rye bread. An essential place for pigs like me to stop. Their cheese is very very good.

CHARBONNEL ET WALKER. I do have to agree with their slightly off-putting statement that they make probably the best chocolates in the world. The vanilla caramels are superb, as is the fudge. The rose and violet creams tend to be rather stale (the only ones that are). They produce some object called a cartouche – lemon and mint flavours, of which the mint or green-foil-wrapped one is better – which is a gem: a cylinder of the purest richest finest chocolate into which has been deposited a tiny sweetie! Yum . . . Peppermints très good too. Their tablets of chocolate are as good as F & M's if not better. Very reliable. I used to have a standing order for caramels but elected to pull myself together. Now the little spaniel gets a tablet from them when he goes into kennels. Not as sweet as Godiva chocolates.

FERN'S COFFEE & TEA. An old shop, famous for the rudeness of its staff and, slightly more important, its coffee – blends especially. I know nothing about tea and almost as little about coffee, but if you confess to supreme ignorance the moment you come in they will explain the complexities of roasting coffee and the best ways to make it.

FORTNUM & MASON. Their frozen – don't shriek! – quails in raisin sauce is a great standby. I don't believe their cheese or smoked salmon is anything to write home – or to you – about, but their turtle soup and pickles and chutneys are inordinately fine. Foie gras cheaper I think at Harrods. Chocolates are very very good indeed, though their truffles go almost before luncheon; if, if one can get there when they come down from the kitchen, you are in for really a truffle completely on par with the 100% perfect Hobbs champagne truffle. These F & M truffles set the standard until a few months ago and I am very sad they have fallen to #2½. What else do I buy there? White grapes and limes. They turn a blind eye when a spaniel walks in. Their own brand whisky is very good.

HARRODS. The only thing I could add is that the new French cheese they stock has changed my life. There is no way I could go on breathing if Boule de Paris absented itself from its stock. Their petits fours are I D E A L. Oh dear, I have now made myself quite ill. Also they have smoked quail and very reasonable foie gras – two things I depend on. (Also, a kennel for little dogs to sleep in while very greedy masters pig up.)

WOOLWORTH'S. Don't laugh – the fine food section is very good. Most of their things come from Foodfinders, but they are selected with care. They were the shop in London that sold French brown sugar cubes (loved by Janetta). Also the best place for dog food.

Some English gentlemen look to their club as a second home; Stanley looked to Claridge's Hotel (clubs don't pay enough attention to food). Here he had drinks and dined several times a week, alone or with friends, twice took a suite for himself over the Christmas holidays (a "bargain" at that season, he said), even had his hair cut ("they have the only barber shop where I can take the dog *and* have a good lunch").

Ensconced for the holidays in a suite of rooms each of which was larger than his entire flat, Stanley invited friends to drop in at leisure for drinks. Some who came felt sorry for him, alone in a hotel on a family holiday; others knew he was in his element. "Claridge's excused me from my usual deep Christmas depression," he wrote Victoria Glendinning:

I generally leave town, but this year I simply couldn't face

Heathrow or anything more radical than a taxi. Of course I packed badly, but I vowed not to come home for anything, and on the way there I remembered that I had forgotten my toothbrush. Stop. Go into grandest chemist ever and all they had were gold t-brushes. Flinch! Then they found one, for a mere snip of £5 and when I got to my room I unpacked it and found it was the vulgarest gold torso of a too thin lady. So much for rules! And I did keep one television – there were three originally littered about the place – and I did see *Citizen Kane* which was really dazzling. It ought to be made mandatory viewing for every writer who subscribes to more rather than less in style. And there was lovely room service . . .[4]

Of which he made good use. Selina Hastings recalls arriving one afternoon: "I went up in the lift and didn't know which of those long corridors led to his suite, but I looked to the left and there was a trolley with a silver bucket and an empty bottle of champagne and this stack of plates, and I thought, 'That must be Stanley.' "

After their drink and despite the evidence of recent food deliveries, Stanley told Selina he was hungry and wanted "a bite to eat before going out to dinner":

So we went down and he ordered a sort of minestrone soup. When it was put in front of him he took a mouthful and went "UUUUUUUGH!" I said "Stanley, what's the matter? Is there a toad in it or something?" And he said, "OOOOOOgh. Frozen peas!" He called the waiter over and said, "Would you find out from the chef whether he's using frozen peas in the soup." And the waiter said, "Oh yes, Mr. Olson, I'm afraid the chef did use frozen peas because it's impossible to get fresh peas in December." Stanley said "I thought so" and just pushed it away. Not only was he the only person who would notice this, he was the only person who would mind.

If frozen peas at Claridge's offended his finicky tastebuds, imagine his horror when confronted with the standard rubber-chicken-greasy-peas menu served up at catered dinner meetings. When Sybille Bedford proposed him for membership in PEN (the international organization of poets, essayists, novelists), she let herself in for trouble:

> He was good about donations and would sit in the front row and be very supporting whenever I spoke at meetings. But we have quarterly dinners to talk about prisoners of conscience, and the food is appalling. And Stanley wrote a letter and *said* the food was appalling and the waitresses were wrong. Now the waitresses *are* dreadful; they sort of push away your plate before you've even eaten. But it made an awful uproar, which I was responsible for.

The PEN officers, rightly angered at being held to restaurant standards while doing their human-rights work, would hardly have been mollified by the knowledge that he was just as picky about dinner parties at Claridge's. "With Stanley everything, every detail [of a party], had to be different, exceptional," says Selina Hastings:

> For instance, Claridge's didn't have the right shaped tables. They had round tables, they had oval tables, and they had oblong tables. But Stanley wanted an absolutely square table. So this had to be constructed. Then they didn't have the right weight of damask tablecloths, so that had to be straightened out. Then he didn't think that anything on their enormous menu was right, so he had to have a pudding invented. He once took me into the kitchens to meet his friend the chef, and they were discussing this great sort of bombe which was chocolate and cream and . . . I mean it was so rich it was obscene! And Stanley very sweetly called it after me because I'd finished my book, and it was known as "Bombe Selina."

On April 10, 1986, *Sargent*'s official publication date,

Stanley planned to host the perfect celebration: he would book the "Orangery," a small private dining room at Claridge's, and invite a dozen friends for lunch. Complications with the guest list proved far more troublesome than the table-shape-and-napery problems of the "Bombe Selina" event, as his letter to the restaurant manager makes clear:

Dear Mr. [Bruno] Rotti: Of course it will come as no surprise to you that there is a baby crisis brewing – I have the unwinning talent of provoking confusion over every detail of my life: nothing is too simple to avoid it. So will you please sit down.

The current tabulation of those invited to the Orangery trough comes to 14! God help us, or at least a swift diet all round. Not that it matters, but the fault came as follows: one said she would be abroad, then changed her plans and thus could not be disinvited. That threw the numbers out – to 11; another man. Then a wife of one of the prime guests WAS going to be in town, after all, and hey presto, we are up to 13! Need I go on? Goodness, isn't the path to pleasure difficult? What can we – I like that! "we" indeed – do? Have a tight squeeze? Pray influenza sweeps London a few days before? What?

And if you think this is a problem, wait until we get to the menu. I will send you a bottle of headache tablets as prep. You might do well to warn both Mr. Berger and Mr. Lesnik that all their powers of tolerance will be sorely stretched. Perhaps all three of you ought to plan a holiday from the 11th? One guest at least is a vegetarian, though fish and game are allowed. I want only simple things, and I mean ultra-simple, for I've a lecture in the afternoon and another dinner party that evening.

Despite this welter of complications, I do at least KNOW one thing: the Claridge's side of things will run like impeccable clock-work. Do you suppose it could be made contagious? Immediately? Please? . . .

And flowers – I did warn you. Your people or mine?

Even I am now getting dizzy over all of this. And I reckon this is enough for the next instalment in the difficulty stakes. I truly pray you are not writing your memoirs.

Yours, a little apologetically . . .

In the end the Olson party numbered eighteen, seated at a table in the middle of the grand dining room, where both host and staff did themselves proud.

Travel, while it stretches the imagination, makes unusual demands on one's flexibility – a trait in rather short supply in Stanley's baggage. His romanticism and wit were at peak form on journeys, as were his gifts for observation and for telling jokes on himself ("Naturally I took the most up-to-date guide, the 1903 Baedeker, and lost the map of Venice the very moment I arrived; hence I was lost for a full eight days.") But journeys also brought to the fore his unyielding perfectionism and his impatience with people and situations that didn't come up to "standards."

He could be incensed to the point of rudeness – "white with passion, blue eyes blazing" – by bad service from a tired old waiter at a restaurant in Egypt, says Frances Partridge,

> and it was no good telling him that it was unfair to hold the place to the service standards of the Ritz. Stanley: "Well, I do. And we don't agree, so let's not talk about it." Frances: "If you had to choose between good food incorrectly served or bad food elegantly presented, which would you prefer?" Stanley, after trying to avoid the issue, said that he would prefer the latter.[5]

He was impaled on the hook of his own standards.

He longed to travel in the grand turn-of-the-century style he imagined from books and films, and certainly his preparatory routine of oiled suitcases, ironed tissue-paper, and outdated guidebooks set the stage splendidly. But once the preparations were completed, he no longer had control; then the inevitable discomforts of modern travel supplanted his fantasies of intense luxury, and he suffered. The clash between his old-fashioned expectations and the more commonplace realities precipitated what came to be called Spoiled Brat Syndrome, with symptoms – irritability, impatience, arrogance and, sometimes, downright incivility – that only the most loving of travel companions could excuse.

He was aware of his narcissism ("So you see I am yet again closeted, sheltered and pandered to," he wrote, after detailing the pleasures of being the Parladés' houseguest in Spain),[6] but seemed helpless to deal with it. When a tour escort, during a get-acquainted chat, saw "Dr Stanley Olson" listed on the registration form and asked, "And what are you a doctor of?" Stanley replied, "Of complaining, I suppose." (He used the title "Dr" frequently, though the English rarely do; "I get better service when I put that down," he told Frances.)

The best way to ward off Spoiled Brat Syndrome was to minimize the intrusions of modernity, and maximize privacy and luxury. Whenever possible, he crossed the Atlantic by ocean liner. He said it was "very like staying at a superior floating health resort where the view might be slightly monotonous but the regime is unashamedly sybaritic." Best of all, "only six consecutive hours out of 24 are clear of some meal."[7]

Shorter journeys could also be reasonably comfortable, so long as he made his own arrangements. When Robert Kee and Sue Baring invited Stanley to accompany them to Venice one Christmas, they were neither surprised nor insulted when he rejected their flight-and-hotel package and made his own bookings. "Typical Stanley," they said, glad of the pleasure of his company under whatever eccentric conditions. He arrived by first-class train (no charter flight for him, if you please) and checked in at the Danieli. They were booked at an equally fine hotel, by all accounts, but it did not quite come up to Stanley's standard of luxury. Years before, he had raved to Arlene about the Danieli providing "the best hotel-room I have ever been in, save perhaps for the Madrid Ritz":

> [It] had fine 18th century furniture, pure linen sheets which were changed three times a day, a pure feather mattress and a bed-frame of such beauty I can't hope to describe it. It was a proper single room, and was hung with silk brocade that matched the bed-cover and chair perfectly. Lovely silk carpet. A stupendous view.

And he had plenty of time to enjoy it:

> Alas, I fell ill [on] the third day and was dogged by a complete want of energy. . . . The visit from the Venetian doctor was like something out of a Rossini opera. His surgery was closed and he clearly called at the chemist's on the way and bought a stethoscope. But you can imagine the confidence it inspired when he opened his bag and had to take the cellophane off his instruments. He obviously had learned English (!) in Brooklyn because his first words were: "OK, wassamattah" (please intone a slight Italian accent). Otherwise he was astonishingly conscientious and very sensible. And, I feel perfectly well to-day. He told me to give up drink which is rather a fine feature of his regime, and I have.

"Stanley ought never to have gone on a tour. Truly he needed to be on his own," says Frances Partridge, reflecting on her trip to Egypt, in 1980, with Stanley and Janetta and Jaime Parladé. None of them were keen on a package tour, but it seemed the only way they could get bookings for what they wanted to do and see. Stanley was beginning in earnest his Sargent research, and longed to go "steaming up the Nile" as JSS had done. So strong was his desire to visit

Egypt, it even overrode his terror of snakes (he feared them enough to ask Selina Hastings never to wear her silver belt with serpent-shaped clasp when he was around). He would keep a diary, of course, and try to find a magazine to publish it; his entry in the catalogue of traveler's tales of the Nile might even bring in enough money to cover his bar bill.

EGYPT DIARY[8]

Sunday: Cairo. The first instructions we get on Egyptian soil are disquieting: we are to refrain from drinking tap-water. It is pure Nile, with some unsavoury additives. No ice (frozen Nile). No fresh raw vegetables (washed in Nile). And no milk (unpasteurised Nile).

The minute I get to the hotel I ask for a huge vodka and tonic *with ice*. I do not think I am a good traveller. Yet when I call down for a bottle of Evian, it arrives without a cap. Evian is probably pure Seine anyway.

None of this dampens my excitement: the first glimpse of Cairo has done that. As a town it is a complete mess. The noise is appalling, the filth ... Is this the land of the Pharaohs?

Cairo was once great, and even became great again, but today all hope seems lost. Where are those travel-brochure vistas? The great houses are bathed in light and guarded by armed soldiers. There is no organisation to the streets and the buildings look as if they have turned their backs on the Nile.

I go to sleep reading about the Eighteenth Dynasty, feeling no closer to it in Egypt than I did back in London.

Monday: Cairo. Every tourist in the city must have chosen this morning to visit the museum. We are given a rudimentary outline of three thousand years' history in twelve minutes. Our guide makes it boring in the extreme, which can only be considered a real achievement. I also feel that this force-feeding of information is quite superfluous, especially as I am armed with the 1911 *Encyclopaedia Britannica* entry for Egypt and the 1929 edition of Baedeker.

I notice that our guide has the unfortunate habit of referring to the "Revolution". I turn to Frances (who is using the even more modern 1909 Macmillan guide). She nods sagely and says 1952 – when Farouk slipped off the throne. I foresee that my eccentric literature is going to cause a lot of difficulties.

Entry into the museum is like entry into Egypt: little short of pure chaos. The idea of roaming through this place in a pack is repellent and I go off alone. The guards are very friendly. Too friendly. They try to engage one in conversation and, worse, they want to point out the treasures in their precinct. It is just too rude not to show some attention. Therefore I am conducted to a curtained grille.

"Want to see something special?" Guard asks with an inordinately wide grin displaying quite a lot of golden teeth. I nod. "Rameses II! Here! Look!" The curtain is thrown back and I peer through the grille. All I can see is a wooden packing crate. I turn to the guard who is looking round in the most suspicious manner. His hand is out. '*Baqshish!*'

A tip for lifting a curtain? I nod, disbelieving, and pull out a note. I later learn that I have given him the equivalent of £1. Egyptian money is too perplexing. There are no coins and the notes are so old that the ink has rubbed off. Thus one doles out *baqshish* in ludicrously huge amounts.

We have been asked to take our meals in the hotel. It is thought that this will prove a mild form of insurance against the dreaded Nile Stomach. The food, however, is so atrocious that we are very safe. Only the cold hors d'oeuvres, which are strictly proscribed, look inviting. I weigh the predicament: I can't eat what I want and it is impossible to eat what is allowed.

I rush to the hors d'oeuvres: pickled onions, stuffed courgettes, artichokes, lime-green cucumbers, tomatoes – wonderful-looking things of perfect freshness. I am certain they have all been lounging about in Nile water, lapping it up.

On going to bed I turn off the light, knowing full well it will be back on any second for an intemperate rush to the lavatory.

Tuesday: Saqqarah, Gizah. A blameless night. No Nile eruptions. But I do see it would have been appalling to miss the pyramids because of a tomato. I had been warned that Saqqarah, with its famous step pyramid, would be one of the high points of my visit. It was completely blotted out by a terrific row with our guide, who takes a very uncharitable line with those of us who do not wish to be school children and so do not wish to tag after every one of her uninspiring words.

I had always thought that the pyramids were invented exclusively for the postcard trade. I did not expect them to come up to expectation. They surpassed it. The clear blue sky helps. The wonderful light which is refracted into impressive angles of shade helps. The desert helps. Everything about them is stunning. I am deeply impressed.

And I am deeply distressed by the chronic pestering from coachmen, drivers, men on top of camels, boys on donkeys. '*Baqshish!* Guide? Camel ride? Photo of me? *Baqshish!*' The entreaties are very persistent. Baedeker is very severe indeed about these people; I am hopeless and they are maddening.

I am surprised to learn that Gizah, as well as Luxor and Aswan, were health resorts, especially for people with lung ailments. The dust here which sweeps up from the desert in wholesale quantities cannot have been good for unhealthy lungs. And I note that everyone in Egypt appears to cough a good deal.

Wednesday: Cairo, Luxor. We are called at 4 a.m. in order to wait three hours at the airport until our flight goes to Luxor. Our plane is held up because some French notable and his wife have to be given a send-off. Officials file out of a bus and line up. Photographers snap away. Handshakes all round, and finally they mount the steps. Then all of a sudden turn back. They have almost got on the wrong plane. This does not inspire confidence.

The moment we get out at Luxor the mood changes. The change from Cairo is radical. This is Egypt! At last!

We are herded into a minute conveyance which takes us to our boat, parked on the Nile just below the majestic Winter Palace Hotel. All the romance of Egypt blossoms on that stretch of road beside the Nile. Donkey carts, camels, shiny horse-drawn carriages festooned with mountains of rich, clover-like weeds for the horse, bells jangling, and ruins: the Temple of Luxor. This is what we have come thousands of miles to see.

I am greatly excited. I want a drink to celebrate the beauty of the place. My elation drops when I look at my watch. It is 9.15 a.m.

The Nile is not crystal clear; it wasn't even in Baedeker's day, so where *that* fiction originated is anyone's guess. But it is beautiful, and much wider than I expected. The western side of Thebes, the Valley of the Tombs of the Kings, is far away. All we can see is a fertile green line, dominated by a dusty pink mountain range. This must be the most beautiful river in the world, and if anyone were to have told me that I would have been stunned by a river, I would have been stunned. And while I am on the subject, why am I wearing out so many superlatives? I blame Egypt for this intemperance.

Our boat, the M.S. *Triton*, is wonderful. It has seen many a decade's service, with that gentle, worn feeling and the faint fragrance of years of wood polish and cigarette smoke (French cigarette smoke, I notice). The staterooms are ample, but the doors do not lock, and in a country whose national pastime is the hunt for *baqshish* this is more than a little disquieting.

The dining room is presided over by a towering man with petrifying eyes, attired in a get-up straight out of the opera, complete with turban and striped satin robe. We call him The Sultan. The entire boat dances to his tune. He is legendary up and down the Nile. We sit where he tells us and eat what he gives us.

All the waiters are very round. One is a perfect sphere; either the food is delicious or the leftovers substantial. The menu, posted outside the dining room, reveals that it is both substantial and pretentious.

The French have been here before us, and to our dismay we learn that they are to join us at midnight. I also discover that it is impossible to drink warm vodka, even when flavoured by the delicious Egyptian limes.

We go to the English-language sound-and-light show at Karnak. The entire population of London and New York are there. The light is glorious; the sound ghastly. The BBC voice is not comfortable here. My three companions and I elect to keep quiet about our opinion in order not to make ourselves totally odious to tour-life; the general reaction to it, we learn, is ecstatic. I will never make a good tour-member.

Thursday: Luxor, Dendera. This is an odd country: we are going up the Nile to Lower Egypt, and in a few days we will be going down the Nile to Upper Egypt. It has not been easy for me to master this rudimentary detail. I never budge without a map, but I never know where we are.

The gentle thud of the engines began at 6 a.m. which was very exciting, especially as it forced me to look at the sunrise. It is justifiably famous. The banks of the Nile are relentlessly beautiful. I find it hard to comprehend just how it manages to be so astonishing all the time. Children rush to the edge of the river, waving and shouting. This performance never lets up as we steam along, which makes an afternoon nap unthinkable.

The hours we keep are very trying. We disembark to see temples at cruelly uncivilised hours, and thus tempers are slightly frayed by lunchtime. I am told by Frances that my complete lack of congeniality with the tour-members is arrogant. And all the while I thought I was doing them a service by keeping apart. There is another great row, and I refuse to go down to luncheon. By dinner that night I am dubbed [by Jaime] "a spoiled brat".

Friday: Dendera, Abydos, Luxor. Our number is greatly decreased by Nile Stomach. It seems that the ill ones have scrupulously adhered to the dietary restrictions, but have failed to be sensible about drink. The buzz about their illness is really only a buzz about hangovers. I ungallantly point out that the ones laid low with illness are the very ones who were seen kissing The Sultan. My reputation for arrogance climbs.

More serious, however, is the coughing and sneezing going on among the passengers. Hardly surprising: each time we disembark it is freezing, and by the time we return to the boat it is simply roasting. The swift change in temperature is not beneficial in the least.

Our boat stops about a mile outside Luxor. This navigational detail is infuriating. We had hoped to desert The Sultan and dine at the Winter Palace Hotel where, we have learned, they are filming some mystery about the tomb of King Tut. I mean, they were filming; the star cannot be found.

The Sultan gives us a huge grin as we walk into the dining room on the boat. We are told that the hotel food in Luxor is execrable and that the dining room at the Winter Palace has precisely the same effect as negative fly-paper for the poor souls who are forced to eat there. So it is lucky for us that we have not disembarked.

Lucky for another reason, too: the French have somehow managed to get off to go to the French-language sound-and-light. Their absence from the dining room proves how annoying their presence has been. Overhearing French is not, no matter how much romantics like to dither over the fact, a pleasant experience. The French have an affection for boredom that cannot be explained. No conversation ever outpaces civilities; by the time all those interrogative *Comments?* have been shuffled about it is time for coffee in the salon. No wonder we use French exclusively as menu-language.

Saturday: Luxor. We seem to be entertaining a huge

mosquito colony. Last night they selected my stateroom for their entertainment and turned me into their refreshment. I am driven to distraction by their bites. My fingers and toes have been turned into minor mountain ranges. A mosquito bite on the soles of the feet is perhaps rivalled only by Chinese water-torture.

Thus I cannot concentrate on what Luxor Lola, our guide, is saying. She bears a striking resemblance to Leontyne Price, and is about as sultry as can be. Her demeanour is probably exaggerated to cover up her peculiar mastery of English. I believe she has learned her speeches phonetically and really hasn't the slightest idea of what she is saying. All questions are answered with a recital of an inappropriate portion of the speech she has just reeled off.

Karnak is more impressive by daylight. It shows up Rameses II's additions as being singularly vulgar. We are apparently getting very sophisticated about all things Egyptian.

In the afternoon we go to the market. It is a nightmare of filth and smells, and the custom of bartering is most unpleasant. The first price quoted, which we are told to halve, seems so reasonable that I cannot bring myself to haggle. But the shopkeepers look so dejected when their wares are handed over without a fight that I am forced to make some pretense at argument. No matter what price one pays, there is always the gnawing thought that it should have been less.

Sunday: Luxor. A marathon day on the west bank of the Nile. It is impossible to visit the Valley of the Tombs of the Kings later than 7 a.m., so we are up and out at 6. We are given all the mystic rigmarole attached to King Tut's tomb and have to elbow our way through about a hundred Italians to see anything. This massive attendance on the dead gives me an unpleasant sense of claustrophobia.

Even Luxor Lola passes up the chance to descend into Seti's tomb, blaming her heart. But I catch her stuffing her mouth with stale cakes at the rest-house. She giggles and suggests that some of our number might like to walk over the parched white limestone mountains that separate the Valley of the Kings and Queen Hapshepsut's temple. I see her jaw drop, full of yellow cake, when two of us start out.

She swiftly waddles out and gets us a guide. And good thing she did; there are about five distinct paths and my sense of direction would have got us to walk in a perfect circle. We scale the mountain at a crack pace, and I look down at the Valley, secretly hoping that some of our party will be watching this brave, and totally unexpected, display of energy.

The soft cream-coloured limestone is formed in a series of sheer cliff-faces and supple waves, reflecting the light in a manner difficult to describe. It is utterly barren, lifeless – a detail which is heightened by silky blue sky.

The higher we get, the more I notice unsettling symptoms. I think I suffer from vertigo. I am hundreds of feet above the Valley of the Kings, peering across to the Nile and Luxor and Karnak, and I cannot look down! The paths are not in any way dangerous, yet they skirt the very edge. I have serious doubts about my sanity.

We are handed from guide to guide, each with one thing on his mind – *baqshish*. We have not seen another living soul save these guides, and this fact coupled with the unexpected beauty of the walk, makes our climb and descent the most pleasant excursion we have done in Egypt.

I have also become very sunburnt, and just try scratching a mosquito bite on burnt skin! I decline to bestir myself at the next three stops, saving all my energy for the stairs up to the bar in the boat. I have come to believe that massive quantities of alcohol will kill any germ the Nile can dish out. It is not a theory shared by the more moderate members of our group.

Monday: Esna, Aswan. We have to leave the boat because some lock on the Nile is being repaired. Thus we cannot sail to Aswan and must go overland. We file into the tiny bus, and are then asked to get out again because there is a flat tyre. And of course the jack has disappeared. The whole population of Esna has gathered to watch the momentous change of tyre. All the while the French are playing bridge and sunning themselves on the deck of the boat. The cook has tossed a particularly luscious bone to one of the stray dogs on the quay. The instant he picks it up another dog flies at him and steals the bone.

By the time the bus is ready, four of our party have wandered off. It is always the same four who are determined to show us that they are more interested in everything than anyone else. I suppress some very sarcastic thoughts.

Riding in that bus is a misery after the ample leisure of the boat. Luxor Lola bounces about in the back, fanning herself in a highly aggressive manner.

The hotel at Aswan possesses dangerous leanings towards grandeur and is knee-deep in filth. The *table d'hôte* surpasses the most nimble imagination. It is one thing to float on the Nile; it is quite another to have it dished up as soup.

Tuesday: Aswan. There is an expedition to some far-off temple. The mere sight of that bus keeps us where we are. Only the Famous Four venture forth, as might have been expected. I tell myself that it is a mere Ptolemaic temple – too recent for my tastes.

Two of us walk along the banks of the Nile to the huge market. I am after rag rugs and cotton for shirting. Ladies are struggling with energetic turkeys, children are pleading for rather revolting pink sugar statues we have seen everywhere and will probably regret not buying. The rag rugs are amazingly cheap and pretty, but heavy. I get, after a great deal of carry-on, five. My suitcase, however, is unwilling to accommodate them.

The things our tour has been buying! Some astonishingly vulgar copies of the god Horus wearing the double crown of Egypt, small badly carved wooden mummies, and other "antiques" surreptitiously unwrapped in an admirably conspiratorial fashion. Even Luxor Lola had to put a stop to it at one point.

We move to the Cataract Hotel. This is where Agatha Christie wrote *Death on the Nile* – and no wonder. It must have one of the most ravishing views in all of Egypt, and that's saying something. The Nile is very clear here. The pitched sails of the boats are snow white. Everything is perfect.

I cannot sleep for the dust which is virtually thrust into one's room by the high winds. Even discounting the dust, the noises emanating from the loudspeaker on the mosque all night rule out any sleep. This religious shouting has set off the dogs. What a chain of disturbing events!

Wednesday: Aswan, Cairo. In order to get out of Aswan one has to pass the new dam. The Egyptians are very proud of this structure and flock to see it. I cannot invoke the slightest interest. All I can think about is the fact that it's built on a geological fault, that it has caused irreparable damage to the Nile Valley, and that it is crawling with mosquitoes. (And also that if Lake Nasser couldn't be restrained somehow, Egypt would be past-tense in an instant.) I sit with my back to it. We have come to this dam and missed the stunning temple at Philae!

We reach Cairo at 7 p.m. and head for what is considered the very best restaurant: Carroll's. Of course, what is thought good by Egyptian standards is far beneath comprehension anywhere else. (Though I am told that the scale of quality in Tunisia begins at the bottom of the Egyptian and goes down; a cheering thought.)

At Carroll's all the show of fine food is evident. The only problem is the food itself. I order a steak. I demand that it be rare. The trolley is wheeled over, there is a mad flourish with dishes and spoons and one of those flames encased in a silver column that the Café Royal depends upon. We are in for a real dining experience and no mistake. The kindness and attention of the waiters makes the whole thing depressing. The steak is deftly burnt to a cinder, in the grandest possible way. There is a dead fly on the tablecloth and some highly leftover people in the place at this late hour. Muzak is spilling forth with the worst sort of low French love-song, over and over again. The Egyptians seem to love it.

Thursday: Cairo. Our last day in Egypt and a wild frenzy of shopping and sightseeing. We make for the Gayer-Anderson house, a private house clearly put together with an enormous amount of love, money and taste, and then left to the Egyptian government. From that moment on, the contents have been singularly unloved. The decay and neglect are appalling. Lovely carpets once brilliant with colour are now dung-brown. Glass has turned opaque. The furniture has been left to rot in the very place where it had once been polished. The place will, eventually, simply fall down around the shoulders of the guards who spend their time wheedling *baqshish* out of unsuspecting people like us.

I find a lovely shop and buy four dozen handkerchiefs and then drag them to my second visit to the museum. It makes more sense to me the second time around. I am conversant with the Dynasties, the Empires, the Pharaohs, but the guards remain mystifying.

It is late afternoon and fast approaching Mecca time. The mosque blurts out the prayer-call. The guards desert their posts. Benches have to be placed in a direct line, as the crow flies, to that holy place. One nimble guardian of four-thousand-year-old objects raises high a bench, fervently spins it round, and cracks the glass in a display case. I am shocked.

I take another look at the treasures of King Tut's tomb. There is a lot of building and decorating activity going on here – the most visited part of the museum. The officials, in their august wisdom, have selected peach-coloured carpet for the million or so footsteps that will cross it. I watch the workmen laying this carpet. I do not believe my eyes. They lift one side of a case; all the objects shoot down and crash against the glass. They lift the other side. Same thing. On the way out I overhear an official giving a Japanese delegation their choice of Tutankhamen ceremonial footstools. Only in Egypt...

I come back to the hotel. Frances has decided that what we have seen in Egypt for the last ten days is not Art – but History! Now this is a serious charge. I can see that it will become a no-holds-barred debunking campaign. The sight of those glorious things in the museum is very fresh in my mind, and this heretical assertion places a hammer on my enthusiasm. I argue admirably, I think, but unpersuasively. I go to my room, muttering. I have a remedial dose of whisky.

After our experience at the "finest" restaurant in Cairo we decide to dine in the hotel tonight. The tour group have gone off to see a show of belly-dancing. Our aloof quartet have not even been asked, but that is appropriate given the stand-offish way we have behaved. Still, it is wounding not to be able to refuse. We talk about the art/history debacle. We are lined up two against two, and it is true deadlock. What a way to finish a tour of Egypt – we can't even decide how to classify what we have seen.

Friday: Cairo, London. It is not uncomfortable to turn one's back on Cairo, but to leave Egypt is sad. The weather in London is about as different as possible: rain. We haven't seen that for nearly a fortnight.

Five years later, in 1985, the Parladés invited Stanley to join them and a group of Spanish friends for a holiday in Srinagar, Kashmir. There, like a maharajah, he lounged aboard his floating hotel suite (he had a houseboat all to himself; the others shared) while cloth merchants, gem merchants, and tailors sailed over through the lotus flowers to display their wares and take his measurements for garments costing a fraction of what they would in London. He ordered three suits and a dressing gown, all lined with red silk; and "when they tipped little heaps of semiprecious stones in front of him, like a conjuror carefully showing off a trick,"[9] he couldn't resist and bought moonstone, topaz, black star, aquamarine, garnet, alexandrite – all for cufflinks and studs to be made up later by his Burlington Arcade jewelers.

His pleasure at his purchases almost made up for the wretched heat and humidity, but not enough to make him sociable: "Afternoon: Severe case of group-itis and read on my boat," he wrote in his diary. "The Spoiled Brat syndrome is coming on me with a force." Some of the group had gone "for a pic-nic in a hot noisy motor"; still others to spend "a more athletic day – bicycle, ride, swim, etc – fools."

Even when he didn't have heat, humidity and "group-itis" to contend with, Stanley's enthusiasm for outdoor activity was tepid at best. To an American friend planning a winter visit to England he wrote:

> From what you say about the book 240 *Walks and Rambles* I take it you are embarking on an ambitious rustic campaign, which automatically excludes me from [giving] any help: my idea of the country and out-of-doors is Regent's Park or Hyde Park, and that is at the will of canine tyranny. Sorry.[10]

His idea of an "athletic" summer's day was a game of croquet on the lawn at a lovely country house. And it was on just such a day and in just such a setting that he was struck down.

Over several days it had been developing – days of excruciating headache and peak frenzy about the forthcoming American reviews of *Sargent*; Selina Hastings and Gill Coleridge had never seen Stanley so tense. But his talent for "collecting" people had brought him an irresistible invitation: he was to spend the weekend (July 18–20, 1986) as a guest of Lady Anne Tree, sister of the Duke of Devonshire, who had introduced them at Lismore six months before. "Stanley was staying with me in Ireland," the Duke says, "and my sister was staying there, and she was so charmed with him, she asked him to stay with her in Dorset. He had the stroke after he arrived."

Hindsight reveals that the stroke began well before he left home, was in process on the Dorset-bound train (where a fellow guest observed him behaving oddly and wondered if he was on drugs), and manifested itself most directly on Saturday afternoon, during a game of croquet, when he complained that his right hand had gone numb. His condition worsened overnight. On Sunday he was taken to a small private hospital just outside Salisbury, and the Duke received a phone call: "My sister rang me up and said, 'We don't know Stanley very well, we met him at Lismore with you. He's clearly not well. Who should we get in touch with?' And I got hold of Selina Hastings and she went and picked him up."

When Selina arrived at the hospital a few hours later, she found Stanley sitting on his bed wearing shirt and tie and trousers. It seemed odd to see him not wearing a jacket:

> When I came in he started giggling. I used to call him "Stawn" because we thought it sounded French and he didn't like "Stan," but he loved "Stawn." I said, "Come on, Stawn, we have to get into the car. You have to put on your jacket." And the nurse began helping him, because his right arm was helpless. And he was sort of fooling about and giggling and making a pantomime of it. At that stage he could still say quite a lot [and he insisted on going to London, not to the nearest large hospital, in Southampton]. When we got in the car the nurse said, "By the way, if he looks as though he's falling asleep, forget about trying to make London and just go as quickly as you can to the nearest hospital. Don't let him fall asleep."
>
> By this time it was the middle of Sunday afternoon in summer, so the traffic was beginning to build up. He started by being very cheerful. The Queen was away somewhere odd

– she'd gone to open some games, one of her endless foreign tours – and Stanley began saying something about this. He started the sentence "Did you see about the Queen in Lusaka" and then gibberish came out. Not words, just nonsense. And he then began nodding rather hysterically and he tried the sentence again and again, and each time halfway through it just became gibberish. I was rather frightened by this. I tried to sort of jolly him along, talk to him, just chatting. He became more and more silent and I thought he was getting sleepy and I was trying to say "Oh look, Stanley! Look at those cows!" or whatever it was. The traffic was getting solid on the motorway, and I suddenly thought, "I don't know where the nearest hospital is. I haven't the faintest idea. I might waste hours trying to find it, so I must get to London." Just as we got to the outskirts of London, Stanley began rocking backwards and forwards and rolling his head and saying, "Oh, the pain, the pain." He could still say quite a lot of words.

When the nightmare ride finally ended and he was admitted to the Harley Street Clinic (where Selina and the Duke of Devonshire stood as his next-of-kin), Selina rang Gill Coleridge at her weekend cottage in the country, hoping that she might know how to reach Stanley's parents. "Try and find his address book," Gill told her. So she removed his keys from his jacket and went into his flat. "And I remember going through his desk and coming across all these half-eaten boxes of chocolates."

Gill drove in from Suffolk, Selina handed over the address book, and Gill set about finding the real next-of-kin. She waited "until a decent hour in America" and began calling the telephone numbers listed under "Olson" in Stanley's book. "We didn't even know who his doctor was, let alone his parents," she says. "It was an *extraordinary* feeling [to know] someone who knew so many people but that no one knew anything about." Eventually she reached Stanley's mother and told her what had happened. "Then I found the name of a doctor and rang him and he said yes, Stanley was his patient."

Stanley's parents and brother arrived from America on Tuesday afternoon, only a few hours before he lost consciousness. The doctors had by now conducted tests, the results of which made them highly pessimistic; they told the family that Stanley's condition was grave, that he was not likely to survive.

The Olsons decamped to Claridge's, exhausted from their overnight flights, shocked and horrified at the prognosis. Norman suggested that his father call the Albert Einstein College of Medicine, in New York, where he had endowed a chair in cardiology, and get from them the names of the top stroke specialists in England.

Dr Clifford Rose took charge of the unconscious patient next day, had him moved from Harley Street to the Charing Cross Hospital in Hammersmith, and told the family that if Stanley survived the next seventy-two hours he would make it. Arlene and her husband, Stanley Muravchick, M.D. (after her marriage, her brother signed himself "The Fake Dr Stanley"), arrived to join the vigil.

As in those crucial days in 1947 in Akron City Hospital when the premature baby tipped the balance toward life, once again Stanley overcame the odds. Once again there would be months of round-the-clock care, and fears that he might never be able to function independently. But again he would triumph.

"After about a month he could communicate – with body English and his eyes," Norman says, "– enough to make his wishes known. By September he had access to a few 'filler' phrases and curses – 'Never mind' or 'Shit-a-brick' – though he often used them inappropriately." Physical mobility returned gradually, as did his sense of humor. ("Both of us bit our nails," says Susannah Phillips, "and would compete in growing them. So it was very touching when I came to see him in hospital and he proudly showed me his new long nails which he then gestured for me to file down, beaming all the while." Victoria Glendinning was amused and astonished when "Exorbitant!" became "the first sensible word" she heard him utter.)

During all phases of his crisis and the subsequent five-month hospitalization, friends flocked to his side; several came daily (Frances Partridge worried when she caught a cold and had to miss even a day or two). Flowers and cards streamed in from everywhere – even Mrs Carr from the Chatsworth staff wrote to wish him well – and the owners of a restaurant he liked in the King's Road brought him his favorite dishes from their menu. There was no gatekeeper during hospital visiting hours; the friends he had formerly compartmentalized now rubbed shoulders at his bedside, becoming acquainted without benefit of Stanley's introduction. (Other little secrets came to light: a glance at the chart hanging from his bed revealed to Ann Dex that her "same-age" friend was in fact a year older.)

When the initial crisis passed and recovery began, Stanley entered a sort of second childhood, becoming receptive to friends' physical expressions of affection and mothering in a way unimaginable before – almost as if he were compensating for the first year of his life, when the incubator and his tiny size prevented much in the way of hugs and kisses. Before he regained full consciousness, there were times of "little cradlings," Ann says, "when he lay perfectly still and one could sit with him, hold his hands and stroke them gently, like a cat."

Ironically, his love for stories and news and gossip was better satisfied now, when he was speechless, than ever before. A visitor could sit beside his silent form, hold his hand and reveal all sorts of secret troubles; whether Stanley heard or not, could respond or not, his friends drew closer to him. "He was a bucket being filled with confidential information," Victoria Glendinning says, quite certain she wasn't the only visitor who occasionally used her visits to think aloud about private matters.

If he had not been gravely ill in the autumn of 1986, Stanley would have been in America on a book-promotion tour timed to coincide with the opening of the Whitney Museum's Sargent retrospective. Among the flurry of events scheduled in connection with the exhibition was a symposium called "Sargent and American Painting Abroad," in which Stanley and his esteemed Boston University mentor would share the podium – Millicent Bell to lecture on the Sargent/Henry James connection. Instead of celebrating together in New York, Professor Bell visited Stanley in Charing Cross Hospital during the early weeks of his "dreadful disablement":

> It was one of the most moving things I have ever witnessed – the spectacle of that bright, intelligent face with its brilliant eyes that seemed to seize one and express his distress and affection. He embraced me, and tears went down his cheeks, and in the nearly mute imprisonment of his aphasis he was able to utter one word to express his view of the whole thing: "Shit!" He seemed to enjoy anything I could tell him, and would say, from time to time, "More, more!" and seemed intensely appreciative and alive, despite his condition.[11]

By December it had become clear that Stanley was ready to go home; indeed, if he stayed any longer in the hospital his condition might deteriorate. After five months he had mastered the system: all those years at Culver had taught him a thing or two, and now when the nurses sent him upstairs for therapy he was just as likely to go downstairs for ice cream. "The nurses adored him," says Ann Dex, "even though he demanded the most outrageous things and the most amazing degree of attention. He got exactly what he wanted from them, even though he could barely speak." (Within a week after coming home, he ordered a huge chocolate cake from Le Gavroche and made Brigit Appleby drive him to the hospital so he could give it to the nurses.)

Norman, who had come over from California five times in as many months (and would come three or four times a year henceforth), arrived in mid-December to move Stanley back into the mews and to firm up arrangements with the caregivers and helpers who would smooth the transition. An entire staff would be required, from nurse to dog-walker: speech therapist, physiotherapist, housecleaner, meal preparer and more. Ann Dex agreed to be general factotum – Stanley's bookkeeper, social secretary, appointments monitor – and on-site liaison between the Olson family and Stanley's retinue.

Afflicted by serious heart disease and chronic illness themselves, Stanley's parents gave over to Norman respon-sibility for arranging and monitoring Stanley's care. (They would come to London to see him as often as their health permitted, and they and Arlene would contact him regular-ly by telephone.) The father of two sons himself by now, Norman was in a position to exercise the paternal discipline he had sometimes found wanting in Sidney. But rather than sternness, he exhibited toward his brother tenderness, indul-gence, generosity and, above all, respect for his integrity. Without Norman's extraordinary attentiveness – and the financial resources of their parents – Stanley could not have resumed an independent life.

Complete privacy was still a few months off, however. In the beginning he shared his flat with a series of live-in nurses. They were less easily distracted than the busy staff at Charing Cross Hospital, but he managed to get around them (and all successive caretakers) often enough: how else to explain the mysterious and frequent arrival of boxes of chocolates from Charbonnel et Walker?

*

Neither defiance nor denial is of the least use here: one takes arms by learning how to negotiate or navigate a sea of troubles, by becoming a mariner in the seas of one's self. . . . accommodation is concerned with weathering the storm.[12]

Though impatient and irritable about so many minor things of life, Stanley withstood his major adult-life crisis with a patience and good humor verging on heroism. The man whose joy had been to read, write and speak, whose pleasure had been to smoke, drink and eat, could now only speak (barely) and eat (restrictedly). Yet hope remained that in time his way with words would be restored to him. Meanwhile, he would carry on by other means.

Fully mobile except for his right hand, he didn't look like a stroke survivor. Only when he was tired did he drag his right leg a little; otherwise, as Norman says, "he managed to make his gait have a seasoned elegance." Nor did he speak like a stroke survivor. Everything he said sounded normal (if occasionally inappropriate); the problem was that he could say so very little. His store of knowledge and memories remained intact, but the neural pathways from store to speech had been obliterated. His repertoire of stock phrases – "thank you very much," "never mind can't be helped," "typical," "oh shut up!" [to himself], "more news, more stories" – expanded over time, and occasionally, unpredictably, he gave utterance to lengthy complex sentences. But for the most part, "I know but I can't say" was the refrain of the next three years.

Grieved at his loss – and theirs – Stanley's old friends marveled nonetheless at his ability to carry on so gallantly in the face of changed circumstances. "After the stroke," says Robert Kee, "his style remained just the same, and his wish – and I think sometimes his anxiety – to be able to preserve his standards. Obviously it was very difficult, but he didn't seem to drop them at all." Newcomers (he liked being around people who hadn't known him previously) were thoroughly charmed: "I think of him always with absolute delight, and I only met him after his illness," says Judy Thomas, one of several friends he made in the next three years.

Stanley's sweet-tooth and appetite also came through the débâcle unscathed, making it necessary to alert everyone to the new dietary regime. Soon after he was well enough to go out, Selina Hastings and John Saumarez Smith took him to lunch. "We went on a Saturday," she says, "because we thought it would be easier to park near the restaurant:

> We'd been told very severely by his doctor that he was not to have anything sweet, rich, creamy – anything that he liked. We ordered something for him which he didn't in the least want – like grilled chicken and salad. Near the table, by the door of the restaurant, there was a huge trolley full of wonderful desserts. He began looking at it, and then he began pointing at it – he couldn't speak at all about it – and John and I were saying "No, Stanley. Would you like a little fresh fruit?" And he began gesturing and pointing, and I said "You're *not* having it. You're not to have it. Have some fresh fruit and salad." He got more and more agitated and I started getting cross, and then I looked and he wasn't pointing at the trolley at all. He was pointing at a traffic warden who was obviously on the prowl, about to ticket my car!

Mobility and independence rekindled Stanley's passion for shopping and making extravagant purchases. It had been a long while since he had visited his favorite shops, and he found new ones. "He opened charge accounts right and left," says Ann Dex, who paid the bills and then arranged to close the accounts, managing to do so without injuring Stanley's reputation and dignity. But when his old spending patterns threatened to reassert themselves with full vigor, "Mother went over and put her foot down," Arlene says. "And when my mother raised her voice, with that Hungarian temper, my brother Stanley listened." He stuck to his budget from then on. "His tone and voice completely changed when he talked to his mother," Kerstin Williams says, having been present on several occasions when they spoke on the telephone. "He was heartbreaking. She was worried about him and the whole thing was just devastating. As I watched him speak to her he completely changed, he was completely the child."

———

Although Stanley's social calendar was radically reduced, he accepted invitations and went out often. Victoria Glendinning thought him quite brave: "It would have been much easier under the circumstances just to stay at home, I should think," where friends could see him on his own terms, "but he always seemed glad to come to dinner." She never felt anxious about him at parties because he didn't seem embarrassed by his limitations in conversation, was perfectly attentive to what others had to say, and was very amusing. "He'd get tired around ten and have to go home, but he would hug everybody when he left."

Stanley got around quite independently; he had an account with a taxi company and used it liberally. He carried a printed card with his own address, so he could always get home, and when he went to visit friends he had someone print their address on a card that he then handed the driver. It was a good system, giving him autonomy and relieving his friends of a potential burden, although it lent itself to a type of Stanley-mischief that his stroke only intensified, as Selina Hastings learned one afternoon:

> He and I had a writer friend who is extremely ungenerous, and Stanley rather had it in for her. She was not only ungenerous about sharing information with writer colleagues, but she never gave her guests enough to eat. He always thought it was very funny and if he and I went to dine there we had a running joke about it.
>
> After his stroke, when he was getting about by himself

quite well, we were both invited to dine with this lady, and he did the most terrible thing. I'm sure he did it on purpose. I offered to come and pick him up but he was insistent on taking a taxi. I said, "I'll send you type on a postcard with her address." So I wrote it, and on the postcard unfortunately I also wrote: "Dear Stawn, You'd better have a good dinner before you leave home, because we sure as hell won't have enough to eat once we're there."

I had already arrived when I heard his taxi pull up. Stanley came out, rang the bell and our hostess let him in. And then he handed her the postcard, and she read it and was not pleased. And it was made worse by the fact that that evening happened to be an even scantier meal than we'd ever had before there.

So Stanley was wicked! But he wanted to give her a lesson and it did her good. It was very funny. I said something to her like "Oh, it's just a joke Stanley and I have, because he and I always eat too much." Although it was a joke, I think he did mind her stinginess very much.

Stanley's enormous sense of fun never left him; it simply surfaced in new ways. If he could no longer talk very well, then he would hum and sing – loudly – the Hallelujah Chorus, nursery songs, old popular songs, especially when he was riding with friends in a car. "Sometimes he'd have to go 'Dah-de-da' with the lyrics," says Susan Loppert, "but then sometimes he'd come out with all the words." He and Victoria Glendinning made quite a tuneful racket driving home from his favorite Chinese restaurant one evening, with Stanley interrupting to issue occasional route instructions. (He had a remarkable spatial sense now, when before he had always mocked himself for getting lost and taking wrong turnings.) But his sense of fun was stronger than his ability to sustain it; he tired easily, and it was painful to watch. "He would just disappear away from one," Kerstin Williams says. "You could see that he just wanted to be home, he just wanted to lie down, didn't want to be there."

Yet when Stanley awoke in the morning he ran everyone in circles, especially the dog, whose ears he bombarded with affectionate cries of "Sweee-t!" a hundred times a day. "The Second Greatest Spaniel in all the world," Ambrose Cornelius Hornet had arrived at the mews only days after Wuzzo's death and some nine months before Stanley's illness. "Jet black, very quiet, and very playful, he will be wildly spoiled from the start," Stanley wrote, "and has taken to luxury like a duck to water." (Luxury included a basket filled with "2 cashmere pullovers, a week's worth of dirty shirts, 2 pairs of slippers, 2 hot-water bottles, and the grandest health insurance possible.") After the stroke Ambrose brightened his master's days by, among other things, serving as scapegoat; Stanley needed an excuse to shout, and the dog's mischief provided ample opportunity.

It was a three-ring circus at the mews during Stanley's morning energy spurts, but Ann Dex was the ablest of ringmasters. She still had her own artist-management business to run, and Stanley interrupted now more than ever, but she took it in stride; looking after him was not unlike managing yet another performing artist.

On my September 1988 visit to London, I noted in my diary: "Stanley seems far happier and livelier than last year." For one thing, his talent for manipulation, developed and refined over a lifetime, was now paying off. He could get people to do *anything* for him; it was nearly impossible to turn him down. He had numbers of people wrapped around his little finger – Kerstin Williams, for one:

> He told me it was his birthday – he never talked directly about his birthday but he let all of us know in some subtle way – and he said he wanted a party. It was to be at his flat and he wanted the Zervudachis [Nolly and Caroline] to come,

and Sybille Bedford and Frances Partridge – perfectionists! – Caroline has even written cookery books. And I said, "Well, who's cooking it?" and he said: "YOU are."

"Have you got everything there?" I asked. And he was too funny! – he said, "Yeah, sure." And he had nothing – he was very ill and very tired. But he did the menu and we cooked it and we had the most hilarious time.

"He always picked me up," she says, "even when he was ill. If I felt down, I would go and see Stanley. He'd just look at things in a completely different way. He would take away all the things I'd come there worrying about."

Ever something of a character in the neighborhood, now he was free to be a full-blown eccentric if and when he chose. Who would criticize a disabled person, for heaven's sake? Merchants in the Montagu Square-Crawford Street area grew accustomed to Stanley, with spaniel in tow, strolling into their shops and taking center stage. Every day he went to the flower shop for his white-rose boutonnière (which the florist had to place just-so in the antique silver "buttonhole vase" given him by Brigit Appleby and Ann Dex on his fortieth birthday), and every day he popped into the chemist's shop, loudly humming "The Ride of the Valkyries" until the proprietors (whom he called Herr and Frau Drugg) begged for mercy. It was quite an adventure to accompany him on his daily rounds. In my diary I wrote:

Did morning errands with cock-of-the-walk Stanley. He's got a loonyness about him as he goes about the neighborhood, where everyone knows him and waves or stops to chat. He's a little batty here, and I suspect he enjoys having the privilege of behaving so (he acted completely the proper gentleman whenever we left the neighborhood). He wears a rumpled beige silk suit (lapels a bit stained, a casualty of left-handed eating, I imagine), and when I comment on its elegance he twinkles at the absurd luxury of it. It's his sense of the absurd – in life and in himself – that I admire most of all. And I'm very grateful for it, because I think it's kept him going these two years, prevented his suffering rageful fits and abysmal depressions. He's as opinionated and funny as ever.

The cock-of-the-walk became a veritable potentate when he traveled. After Ann Dex and Geoffrey Phillips left London to become innkeepers on the Isle of Wight, they invited Stanley to spend a summer weekend at The Lawyer's Rest. With her usual efficiency Ann made arrangements to ease his journey every step of the way from London; but only Stanley could have stage-managed the scene that unfolded at Portsmouth Harbour railway station when Ann arrived to take him from the train to the island car ferry. "The whole platform had been cleared of people," she says:

> and everyone wondered what was going on, when suddenly there appeared a man dressed in a white linen suit, Panama hat, and tiny, old-fashioned sunglasses. He was in a wheelchair being pushed by one British Rail official, while another official walked alongside carrying his luggage. He looked like royalty in a sedan chair, not a handicapped person in a wheelchair. People stood about wondering who this dignitary might be and whether they should ask for his autograph. The whole entourage followed to the car.

Though most of the time he seemed stalwart and cheerful (and *always* put on the best face for an infrequent visitor like me), he was not immune from anger and depression. Gill Coleridge witnessed them often:

> When he was in hospital, the first thing he said to me, crying, was "Rebecca, Rebecca." And nearly every time I saw him afterwards he would say it. "You will get better, you will write this book," I kept saying to him. "I got you a nine-year contract. You've got plenty of time."
> The book was the most important thing to him. He had to believe that he was going to get better and would write

it. When he was finally able to go downstairs to his office again, I'd see the desperation and sadness. He'd slam the file drawers [that held the Rebecca West papers] and he would cry, "Can't read, can't read."

And within moments of amusing his luncheon companions by pointing to the pastry trolley/traffic warden, he touched them to the quick by asking that they stop at the London Library, which they were about to pass in the car:

> He said he would like to go in, would like to go round the room in which he had done most of the research for his books. We waited for him in the lobby. When he came back, the tears came down. He [indicated] that he had traced his finger round the wall. And as he went round – there was his life, there was the library, there was so much![13]

Stanley's speech therapist saw him in circumstances where no amount of manipulative talent could conceal his impairment; the master manipulator was himself being manipulated by the electronic circuitry of his brain. (He still had seizures despite medication to prevent them.) Excerpts from the therapist's reports to his parents make a sad counterpoint to the old Culver reports from the Colonel:

> He is unable to hold a fluent conversation, write a message or read a paragraph. . . . His difficulty [in conversation] is one of access and retrieval of the word and not a loss of knowledge. . . . He is still unable to attempt to read aloud nor is he able to read a sentence or passage silently. . . . Although he has progressed a great deal from his initial illness, it does seem tediously slow to him and it is understandable that he finds it difficult to maintain high levels of motivation at all times.[14]

In the autumn of 1988, when Stanley seemed to me livelier and happier than before, he had just been given a new lease of hope: he was about to start school, and for once in his life was excited about attending classes. The City Dysphasic Group had accepted him into their renowned rehabilitation program; if he was ever to learn to speak, read and write, this was the place it would happen.

But it didn't. A year later when I visited, in October 1989, he still couldn't read or write, and his computer with mouse and "talking" software seemed only to frustrate him. Oral communication was easier, however; now he could establish fairly quickly the context of what he wished to say, and his conversation partner could then zero in on the specifics with a short series of questions. But when I arrived he wasn't talking much; he was very tired – "under the weather," Wylda said. (Wylda Millis, who lived around the corner from the mews, had taken over Ann Dex's role for the past ten months; a Cordon Bleu-trained cook, she easily won Stanley's favor.) There had been flu and then a series of colds; he had even missed a few days of school, she said.

After a nap he perked up noticeably, and I invited him to come for *tapas* at a Spanish restaurant I'd heard about nearby. We decided to walk, despite the brisk, changeable weather. As we proceeded along the Edgware Road, the temperature dropped and Stanley ogled with curious and covetous eyes my bright blue fingerless gloves – the kind that London greengrocers wear in winter when selling vegetables out of doors. Incongruous as they looked with his conservative gray garb, he adored them and refused to give them back, even when fur-lined black leather gloves were found in his pockets.

Next morning, as we waited in his office for the car to pick him up for school, he reached up to retrieve a hatbox from a high shelf. He took out a black top hat (lined with red silk, of course) and placed it on my head with a delighted chuckle. "Did you wear it to meet the Queen?" I asked sarcastically, fingering the archaic ceremonial item. "Yes," he replied with a haughty twinkle, as if I should have known. Only Stanley, I thought, would commandeer greengrocer's gloves and atone for it with a gentleman's top hat. It was our last exchange.

That [he wished for death] I should deny, but I would admit that he always had a distaste for life when it lacked splendour, colour, pace, spirit, panache, style, idiosyncrasy . . . He was like the owner of a once splendid house, now isolated in a declining neighbourhood and past repair, who decides to leave.[15]

At midday on Saturday, December 9, 1989, Susan Loppert and Judy Thomas called Stanley to remind him of his standing invitation to their annual Christmas Eve party. Equivocating perhaps because of his lingering cold, more likely because he was amassing Christmas invitations by the handful and wanted to select the most appealing when the time came, Stanley replied: "Pencil me in." A new phrase in his repertoire, they thought. Encouraging.

Very late that night a neighbor in the mews heard the cry "My god!" and the thump of a body hitting the floor. This time the stroke was fatal. Death came quickly.

"I rise to speak for the family of Stanley Olson," Norman said, on Sunday, December 17, in a chapel at Golders Green. "We will leave our beloved Stanley in the England that he so loved . . ."

And so began Stanley's final celebration, the one party about which he would never learn by pleading "More news! More *stories!*" as he had done so often during the last three years. Low-keyed, dignified, elegant – with gale-force wind accompaniment, then a streak or two of sunshine – the funeral service included most of the things Stanley liked: music (played by Cynthia Millar and Patrick Williams), stories (told by friends), flowers (white), and literature (passages from *Elinor* and *Sargent*, read by Robert Kee). And after, at Claridge's, there was food and drink.

Victoria Glendinning delivered the principal eulogy, celebrating him in words that evoked his presence – "his big, hooded aquamarine eyes, the bow tie, a flash of red silk" – and paid tribute to his quality and standards:

> Stripped of so much – reading, writing, easy talking, travelling – everything that seemingly made him what he was – Stanley became by some miracle of character *more* Stanley, not less. One constant was his talent for pleasure. Stanley was Epicurean: he recognized and preferred the best – in writing, art, building, music, wine, manners, puddings. So, if Heaven is all it's cracked up to be, he'll *be* there. But not otherwise.

When the speakers had finished and Robert Kee reached the end of the service, Norman left his seat to stand alone beside the coffin draped with white flowers. As his lips moved silently – "*Yitgadal, v'yitkadash* . . ." – the audience would not have guessed that he was reciting the Kaddish, the Hebrew prayer for the dead.

Though he would certainly jeer at sentimental grief on his behalf, as Victoria had cautioned us, Stanley might have forgiven our tears at the end of the service by attributing them to Isolde's "Liebestod" from *Tristan* – the transcendental music soaring through the chapel as we filed out into the stormy Sunday morning. He would have had the last laugh anyway: inside the chapel the tape recorder was still running; no one had remembered to switch it off. Two men from the staff, rearranging the chapel for the service to follow immediately upon Stanley's, chatted together in Cockney voices as they flung chairs about: "Any orders for this next one?" "No, just music. Indian music." "That one was a very nice one. Who was the deceased?" "A forty-two-year-old. I think he had something to do with books." The last sound on the tape is of a sitar playing a morning raga.

AFTERWORD

In March 1991, when I came to London and paid a call on Stanley in his final resting place, I learned to my delight that death had not altogether severed Stanley's association with luxury and comfort: his cinerary urn resides in a niche in the Golders Green Columbarium which, it so happens, was designed by Sir Ernest George, architect of Claridge's Hotel.

ACKNOWLEDGMENTS

I wish to express my profound gratitude to Stanley's family – especially Norman Olson and Arlene Olson-Muravchick – without whose trust, cooperation and kindness during these last four years I could not have brought this labor of love to fruition; and to my own family – especially my parents Albert and Janet Schultz – without whose support, both literal and figurative, I would have been unable to undertake that labor in the first place.

I am deeply grateful to the following of Stanley's friends, who granted me hours of their time – in interviews, phone conversations and correspondence – access to their letters and, in many instances, the warmest hospitality: Brigit Appleby, Sue Baring, Millicent Bell, Elmer Bernstein, Tish Lampert Coblentz, the Duke of Devonshire, Joyce Engelson, Henrietta Garnett, Victoria Glendinning, Selina Hastings, Michael Holroyd, Robert Kee, Susan Loppert, Wylda Millis, Janetta Parladé, Geoffrey Phillips, Susannah Phillips, John Saumarez Smith, James O'Shea Wade, Kerstin Williams – and especially Gill Coleridge, Angelica Garnett, and Cynthia Millar.

Others of Stanley's friends and acquaintances whom I thank for their contributions: Susan Campbell, Mirabel Cecil, Algar Cox, Peter Muller, and Judy Thomas. Also helpful were Lord Annan, Howard Gotlieb, Paul Levy, Penelope Levy, David Pryce-Jones, and Jean Strouse. My apologies to those of Stanley's friends whose memories and stories I was unable to tap for this book.

Thank you to those who gave me what I needed at just the right time and in just the right measure (sometimes great): Diana Abrashkin, William Baron, K. K. Beck, David Blum, Sara Blum, Julan Chu, John Erling, Flor Fernandez, Josiah Fisk, Deana Freedman, Kathleen Giblin, Carl Grunfeld, David Hass, Henry Kalman, William Maschmeier, Susan Miller, David Mitchell, Arthur Orrmont, Julie Paschkis, Brenda Peterson, Clyde Reed, Carl Rollyson, David Snider, Harry Thomas, Priscilla Turner, Beth Vesel, Elizabeth Wales – and especially Denise Levertov.

And finally, I owe an inestimable debt to Barbara Erling, Irvine Huck, and my sister, Miriam Grunfeld, for their lovingly tendered critical advice and ever-available emotional support in America; and to their counterparts in England who inspired and encouraged me beyond measure: Frances Partridge, Sybille Bedford, and Ann Dex.

NOTES

PART I: THE AMERICAN YOUTH (1947–1969)

1. Quoted in *Ohio: Matters of Fact*, by Damaine Vonada, Orange Frazer Press, Inc., 1987.
2. Virginia Woolf, *The Voyage Out*, Bantam Classic edition, New York, 1991.
3. Frances Partridge, personal interview, 1991.
4. Cynthia Millar, personal interview, 1991.
5. Peter Muller, telephone interview, 1991.
6. Algar Cox, telephone interview, 1991.
7. Michael Holroyd, letter to Phyllis, 1991.
8. Millicent Bell, letter to Phyllis, 1990.
9. Millicent Bell, letter to Phyllis, 1990.

PART II: THE ENGLISH GENTLEMAN (1969–1989)

BREAKING IN

1. Henry James, *The Tragic Muse* (The Laurel Henry James: Dell Publishing Co., NY), 1961, pp.136–7.
2. Henry James, *The Europeans* (Signet Classics, NY), 1964, p.133.
3. Michael Holroyd, telephone interview, 1991.
4. David Gadd, *The Loving Friends: A Portrait of Bloomsbury* (HBJ, 1974), p.122.
5. Tish Lampert Coblentz, telephone interview, 1991.
6. Michael Holroyd, telephone interview, 1991.
7. *New York Times Book Review*, Sept. 15, 1974.
8. "Summer Fare from England's Literary Gastronomes," June 1979.
9. Stanley's unpublished essay.
10. I am indebted to Michael Holroyd and Selina Hastings for these comments.
11. Frances Partridge, unpublished diary.
12. Frances Partridge, unpublished diary.
13. Frances Partridge, obituary in *The Daily Telegraph*, Dec. 15, 1989.

ARRIVAL

1. Quoted by Mirabel Cecil, "Writer's Mews," *The World of Interiors* magazine, October 1984.
2. Sybille Bedford, personal interview, 1991.
3. I am indebted to Geoffrey Phillips for this anecdote.
4. Gill Coleridge, personal interview, 1991.
5. "People: Extra," by Tim Willis, *Sunday Today*, 20 April 1986.
6. Albert Schultz, Phyllis's father, prepared Stanley's tax returns every year.
7. Published in *Woman's Journal*, February 1980.
8. David Gadd, *The Loving Friends: A Portrait of Bloomsbury* (HBJ, 1974), p.131.
9. Superseded in 1975 by a contract with Dial Press/Wade Publishing.
10. Henry James (from London) to his brother William (in America), 1878;

quoted by Stuart Hampshire, "What the Jameses Knew," *New York Review of Books*, Oct. 10, 1991.

A PERFECT FIT
1. Letter to Phyllis, 1975.
2. Robert Kee, personal interview, 1991.
3. Roy Foster, obituary in *The Guardian*, 19 December 1989.
4. The Duke of Devonshire, personal interview, 1991.
5. Sue Baring, personal interview, 1991.
6. Kerstin Williams, personal interview, 1991.
7. Angelica Garnett, letter to Phyllis, 1992.
8. Frances Partridge, obituary in *The Daily Telegraph*, Dec. 15, 1989.
9. Frances Partridge, personal interview, 1991.
10. Ann Dex, personal interview, 1991.
11. Henrietta Garnett, letter to Phyllis, June 28, 1992, and personal interview, 1993.
12. Henrietta Garnett, letter to Phyllis, June 28, 1992.
13. Henrietta Garnett, letter to Phyllis, June 28, 1992, and personal interview, 1993.
14. Kerstin Williams, personal interview, 1991.
15. Selina Hastings, personal interview, 1991.
16. Robert Kee, personal interview, 1991.
17. The Duke of Devonshire, personal interview, 1991.
18. Kerstin Williams, personal interview, 1991.
19. Mirabel Cecil, "Writer's Mews," *The World of Interiors*, Oct. 1984.
20. Cynthia Millar, personal interview, 1991.
21. Noël Annan, "Folie a Trois," *New York Review of Books*, Nov. 21, 1991.
22. Susannah Phillips, letter to Phyllis, 1991.
23. Susannah Phillips, letter to Phyllis, 1991.
24. Noël Annan, quoting from Naomi B. Levine's *Politics, Religion and Love: The Story of H. H. Asquith, Venetia Stanley and Edwin Montagu, Based on the Life and Letters of Edwin Stanley Montagu*, in *New York Review of Books*, Nov. 21, 1991.
25. Selina Hastings, personal interview, 1991.
26. Ann Dex, personal interview, 1990.
27. Ann Dex, personal interview, 1990.
28. Quoted by Mirabel Cecil in "Writer's Mews," *The World of Interiors*, Oct. 1984.
29. Diary entry, October 1982.
30. Diary entry, October 1982.
31. Mirabel Cecil, "Writer's Mews," *The World of Interiors*, 1984.
32. Letter to Phyllis.
33. Letter to Phyllis, March 10, 1975.
34. Nancy Mitford, *The Pursuit of Love*, Vintage Books, New York, 1982, p.159.
35. Roc Sandford to Stanley.

PART III: THE MAN OF LETTERS
1. Richard Ormond, obituary in *The Daily Telegraph*, Dec. 15, 1989.
2. William Sansom, *Proust*, Thames & Hudson, New York, 1986, p.100.
3. Lytton Strachey, in the preface to *Eminent Victorians*.
4. Letter to Phyllis, March 2, 1980.
5. To Victoria Glendinning, May 8, 1986, after the publication of *Sargent*.

6. Letter to Sybille Bedford, July 15, 1985.
7. John Grigg, *The Listener*, May 29, 1986.
8. Meryle Secrest, *Philadelphia Inquirer*, Aug. 10, 1986.
9. Stanley's jottings, as if in response to an author's questionnaire.
10. *John Singer Sargent: His Portrait*, New York: St. Martin's Press, 1986, p.70.
11. *John Singer Sargent: His Portrait*, New York: St. Martin's Press, 1986, p.212.
12. Letter to Sybille Bedford, July 15, 1985.
13. *Antaeus*, Autumn 1982; *Library Lit: The Best of 1982*, an anthology used extensively by librarians and students of library science.
14. Selina Hastings, personal interview, 1991.
15. Stanley's unpublished essay, written after the January 1979 publication of *Elinor Wylie: A Biography*, Dial Press/James Wade, New York.
16. Avis Berman, *Baltimore Sun*, Feb. 11, 1979.
17. Avis Berman, *Baltimore Sun*, Feb. 11, 1979.
18. Jim Wade to Stanley, Feb. 20, 1976 and Dec. 29, 1975, respectively.
19. Richard Ormond, obituary in *The Daily Telegraph*, Dec. 15, 1989.
20. Gill Coleridge, personal interview, 1991.
21. Letter to Phyllis, Sept. 29, 1979.
22. Letter to Arlene, Sept. 28, 1979.
23. *John Singer Sargent: His Portrait*, New York: St. Martin's Press, 1986, p.203.
24. Letter to Robert Kee, Jan. 27, 1979.
25. Diary entry, March 31, 1985.
26. Diary entry, Jan. 26, 1983.
27. From a draft of lecture notes for series of talks delivered at the National Portrait Gallery in the spring of 1986.
28. Selina Hastings, personal interview, 1991.
29. *John Singer Sargent: His Portrait*, New York: St. Martin's Press, 1986, p.199.
30. Stanley quoted by Meredith Etherington-Smith in *W*, June 30–July 7, 1986.
31. Frances Partridge, letter to Stanley, Nov. 17, 1980.
32. Stanley to Phyllis.
33. *John Singer Sargent: His Portrait*, New York: St. Martin's Press, 1986, p.14.
34. Joyce Engelson, personal interview, 1991.
35. Letter to Phyllis, June 28, 1986.
36. Postcard to Phyllis.
37. The Duke of Devonshire, personal interview, 1991.
38. Meredith Etherington-Smith, *W*, June 30–July 7, 1986.
39. Letter to Phyllis, June 28, 1986.
40. Letter to Phyllis, June 28, 1986.
41. Roger Kimball, *New York Times Book Review*, August 24, 1986, p.2.
42. Letter to Jim Wade, 19 May 1975.
43. Rebecca West, publicity copy for The Dial Press announcement of *Elinor Wylie: A Biography*, December 1978.
44. Letter to parents, July 1978.
45. *Rebecca West: A Life*, Alfred A. Knopf, New York, 1987.
46. Gill Coleridge, personal interview, 1991.
47. Frances Partridge, personal interview, 1991.
48. Letter to Jim Wade – 28 May 1975.
49. Rebecca West, as quoted in Stanley's diary.
50. Gill Coleridge, personal interview, 1991.
51. Victoria Glendinning, personal interview, 1991.
52. Victoria Glendinning, personal interview, 1991.
53. Gill Coleridge, personal interview, 1991.

54. To Victoria Glendinning, 26 June 1986.
55. *London Portrait* magazine, March 1986.

PART IV: THE SYBARITE: A HEADLONG RUSH TO DOOM
1. Kerstin Williams, personal interview, 1991.
2. Attributed (by Elizabeth David) to novelist Norman Douglas and told to Sybille Bedford.
3. Excerpt from article in *Woman's Journal*, May 1980.
4. Letter to Victoria Glendinning, Jan. 3, 1986.
5. Frances Partridge, unpublished diary entry.
6. Letter to Phyllis, Sept. 29, 1979.
7. "A Moveable Feast on the Ocean Wave," *The Mail on Sunday*, Sept. 26, 1982.
8. Most of the contents of this article were published as "A Traveller's Tale of the Nile," in *Woman's Journal*, October 1980.
9. Janetta Parladé, letter to Phyllis, August 1991.
10. Letter to Phyllis, September 1985.
11. Millicent Bell, letter to Phyllis, Dec. 26, 1990.
12. Lawrence Weschler, in "Allegories of Eastern Europe," in *Threepenny Review*, Fall 1990.
13. John Saumarez Smith, personal interview, 1991.
14. Fay Young, M.A., M.C.S.T., September 1988.
15. William Plomer, *Museum Pieces* (Jonathan Cape, London, 1952), p.200.

INDEX